Philip Hyland has been ploughing the employment law field since 1992. He has conducted almost every type of case at Tribunal and some at the CAC. He is particularly interested in discrimination cases and redundancy cases. He has conducted over two hundred and fifty Tribunal hearings.

Renee Pillay is training to be a Solicitor and has a strong interest in workplace behaviour and human rights.

A Practical Guide to the Law of Bullying and Harassment in the Workplace

Second Edition

A Practical Guide to the Law of Bullying and Harassment in the Workplace

Second Edition

Philip Hyland, BA Hons, MA, FRSA, Solicitor

Renee Pillay, BA Hons

Law Brief Publishing

Published 2025 by Law Brief Publishing, an imprint of Law Brief Publishing Ltd
30 The Parks
Minehead
Somerset
TA24 8BT

www.lawbriefpublishing.com

Paperback: 978-1-916698-76-5

To my lovely Jacinta who has provided
inspiration, wisdom, guidance, insight,
and, most importantly, love and support
for more than 35 years.

– Philip

PREFACE

Behaviour in the workplace has taken centre stage. Bad behaviour is being called out. There is no hiding place for bullies, sex pests and harassers.

The law has a long arm for those who abuse their positions of power. Social media turns the spotlight on the abusers, levelling the playing field for the victims.

Individual and corporate reputations can be destroyed in an instant. No industry or sector is immune. Judges, Solicitors and Barristers can and do behave in a bullying and harassing manner. The entertainment industries hidden secrets have been disinfected by the sunlight of publicity. Your business or organisation can be affected by one bad apple.

This book aims to give HR Professionals and Lawyers an easy-to-understand guide to the legal framework that governs workplace behaviour. Understanding, knowledge, insight and awareness are the best foundation to prevent bullying and harassment. This book aims to give that foundation.

The law stated in this book is believed to be accurate and up to date as at 28th February 2025.

Philip Hyland
February 2025

CONTENTS

INTRODUCTION BY PHILIP HYLAND

My first book was a practical guide for handling redundancies.

Since the first edition of this book, I acted for P in her case against Crest Nicholson PLC, a rare case where an employer was found to have contravened the Equality Act by failing to prevent a rape during the course of employment.

This is about workplace bullying and harassment. Workplace conduct and behaviour has never had a higher profile. 2024 will be remembered, amongst other things, for the allegations against Puff Diddy. People in positions of power and prestige have had their workplace behaviour publicly scrutinised. Workplace behaviour took centre stage.

A paper by the British Medical Journal found that the NHS had 20% of staff reporting that they have been bullied to some degree and 43% had witnessed bullying behaviour in the last 6 months. Their conclusion was that bullying is a "persistent problem in health care organisations which has significant negative outcomes for individuals and organisations."[1]

With organisations all striving to improve productivity and efficiency, bullying and harassment can act as a roadblock for organisational improvement. Bullying and harassment not only impacts victims but is a cost to an employer and a cost to the public purse.

A study by Manchester University in 2007 found that workplace bullying cost UK employers £682.5 million annually in terms of absence related cost, with over 100 million lost days of productivity. The study estimated

---

1 Carter M, Thompson N, Crampton P, et al – Workplace Bullying in the UK NHS: a questionnaire and interview study on prevalence, impact and barriers to reporting BMJ Open 2013.

that workplace bullying cost the UK economy over £13.75 billion in 2007 or 1.5% of UK GDP.[2]

This book will provide HR Practitioners with an outline of the legal framework and how that framework has developed as well as providing guidance on the steps employers can take to prevent bullying and harassment in their organisation.

We will also look at the types of defence available to an employer when faced with legal claims from employees or workers alleging bullying or harassment or both.

In my experience as an advisor one of the main problems HR professionals have when dealing with allegations of bullying or harassment is one of definition. It is difficult to define what behaviour or conduct meets the definition.

How does an HR Professional define objectively what behaviour or conduct amounts to bullying or harassment when the evidence is often so subjective?

The HR professionals' first job is to arrange for the evidence to be gathered and analysed when a complaint of alleged harassment is made.

Most cases of gross misconduct have objective evidence to support the allegations. For example, an HR professional will be able to examine the documentary evidence for an allegation of fiddled expenses and come to a conclusion based on that evidence.

Dismissals for theft, failed drugs or alcohol tests, fighting, or breach of health and safety usually have objective evidence available to support any finding of gross misconduct. CCTV evidence, documents or scientific data collected after a test are difficult to deny or dispute. The evidence, if

---

2 The Costs of Workplace Bullying by Sabir I. Giga, Helge Noel, and Duncan Lewis, May 2008.

not clear cut, is often sufficient to enable a finding of gross misconduct based on an objective assessment of the evidence.

Cases of bullying and harassment usually turn on oral evidence. Often that evidence is contested. Often there is a lack of witnesses to corroborate either account of events. The allegations, if proven, will often have far reaching consequences not only for the individual but also for their employer.

It is understandable given the implications that many organisations and their HR Practitioners fudge any issue they are faced with by stating that they cannot make a decision on the veracity of any bullying or harassment allegations as the evidence is not corroborated by other witnesses. HR Practitioners and line managers are all too willing to find allegations not proven where it is one person's word against another's. That can be a cop out and can store up problems further down the line.

What the academic literature shows is that workplace bullying and harassment if allowed to go unchecked can grip an organisation and become institutionalised. The MacPherson report showed that even those tasked with upholding and enforcing the law, the Metropolitan Police, allowed racism to grow unchecked within the ranks. That institutionalisation of behaviour makes it even more difficult for organisations to deal with issues as and when they arise and acts as a barrier for those on the receiving end of bullying or harassing behaviour to report it to management.

If bullying and harassment becomes institutionalised the problems become harder to solve. Those charged with running and managing the organisation can allow a bullying and harassing culture to become the norm.

Where bullying and harassment becomes institutionalised it is difficult for those who are being bullied or harassed to speak out as the procedures to deal with such allegations can be intimidating form of bullying and harassing in themselves and make the situation worse. Those running the procedures are usually those vested with management responsibility and can be subject to group think and not see what is obvious. Bullying and harassment can often be power plays where those in positions of power abuse their power and subject subordinates to bullying or harassing behaviour. Those in power are then tasked with adjudicating any complaints of bullying or harassment made by those in a subordinate position. Those in a subordinate position feel disempowered to raise complaints as they don't trust management to resolve those complaints fairly – this then sets up a vicious circle whereby bullying and harassing behaviour goes unchecked in an organisation.

This book aims to do the following:

1. We will define what bullying is using examples from caselaw. We will look at the legal consequences for an employer that allows bullying to go unchecked. We will look at the type of claims a victim of bullying can make and where they can make them.

2. We will look at how the law defines harassment in statute and how those statutory definitions have been developed and interpreted by the courts and Tribunals. We will look at what sorts of legal action a victim of harassment could take and what courts or Tribunals hear such claims.

3. We will look at the legal consequences for an individual responsible for harassing an employee or worker. We will also look at what liability the individual's employer faces for allowing harassment to take place.

4. We will look at the types of policies and procedures an employer could put in place to prevent bullying and harassment as well as what other practical steps organisations can take to ensure the workplace is respectful and a dignified place to work.

5. We will look at the recent law that came into force on 26 October 2024 that places a legal duty on employers to take reasonable

steps to prevent sexual harassment of your employees or workers. As well as what law is likely to come into 2026 in relation to third party harassment.

6. We will examine what defences are open to an employer when facing legal claims of bullying and harassment.

7. The aim of the book is to give confidence to HR Practitioners and their legal advisers that any allegations of bullying and harassment are dealt with fairly, in accordance with best practice, and thereby protects both the organisation and its staff from the risk of being bullied and harassed and the legal consequences that follow. Ultimately having a workplace free from harassment and bullying will enable an organisation to be more productive and enable all members of the organisation to enjoy their work and be as productive as possible and enable them to reach their full potential.

INTRODUCTION BY RENEE PILLAY

As a young woman navigating the world, I discovered that harassment often lurks just beneath the surface of everyday life. From the moment I stepped into adulthood, I was confronted with unwelcome experiences: catcalling while I walked down a street, sexist comments in social settings, and ultimately, the profound violation of facing sexual harassment in a previous job. These experiences shattered my sense of safety and belonging, transforming what should have been an exciting entry into the professional world into a cautious experience.

The harassment I endured at my earlier job was particularly troubling. It wasn't a one-time event but rather a relentless pattern of behaviour that persisted for months, all stemming from an older colleague who abused his position. I felt trapped in a situation that was foreign to me, unsure of my rights and apprehensive of reporting his inappropriate conduct.

What I experienced is not unique; countless women find themselves in similar situations, feeling isolated and unsure of how to seek help. This book is designed not only to shed light on the pervasive issue of harassment but also to educate, include, and support other victims who may feel powerless whilst dealing with such misconduct.

It is easy, in the legal world, to get caught up in statutes and precedents, forgetting that there are real lives affected. My experience echoes the voices of many women who have been silenced, dismissed, or made to feel powerless in the face of behaviour that should never have been tolerated. By talking about my experience, Phillip and I hope to offer insight into the law surrounding harassment. Working in employment law, I learned not only about my rights but also about the complexities of pursuing justice. The law can be a powerful tool for protecting victims, but it can also be difficult to navigate, particularly for those who are already vulnerable.

In this book, we aim to examine how harassment can be identified in the workplace and the legal avenues available for victims.

CHAPTER ONE

THE LEGAL FRAMEWORK FOR BULLYING CLAIMS

In this chapter we will look at the following:

1. The definition of bullying.

2. The source of the legal rights available to an employee or worker who has been bullied in his or her workplace.

3. The ways those legal rights can be enforced.

1. Sources of definition of what amounts to Bullying

When we look for definition in law of prescribed conduct there are only a limited number of places to look. The sources are limited and well established. The sources are as follows:

1. Acts of Parliament or secondary legislation are a primary source.

2. Caselaw or Codes of Practice issued by ACAS are a secondary source.

3. The third place to look are those organisations with authority in a particular subject or area. Typically reference can be made to academia, academic papers, or research undertaken by those non-departmental public bodies exercising a statutory function such as the Equality and Human Rights Commission or the Health and Safety Executive. Such sources can be and are quoted in legal judgments.

2. Primary sources: Acts of Parliament or Statutory Instruments or Regulations.

Law in the workplace used to be solely governed by the common law of Master and Servant. Leaving aside the gendered terminology, the term servant implies a subservient and unequal position. Politics has played a large part in moving the regulatory landscape on from the rather Upstairs, Downstairs view that if you employed or engaged someone they were your servant. Parliament has elected Members of Parliament with a background in the Trade Union movement. Labour, traditionally, has been on the side of the working person and the name of the party reflects the side it's on in the labour or capital equation.

With Parliament increasingly reflecting the population as a whole rather than landed interests, the majority of the population go to work as opposed to own a business. Parliament has recognised the inequality of bargaining position and has regulated to try to make the playing field more level rather than tilted towards the employers, or capital.

The workplace has become more regulated from the start of the twentieth century onwards. There are laws in place governing many aspects of the working relationship. There are health and safety laws that try to ensure workplaces are safe and healthy for those working in them. No sector of the economy is immune from their reach. Health and safety laws have put rules in place for every type of working environment from working in confined spaces to control of hazardous substances from prescriptive laws on how asbestos should be managed and handled through to six pack regulations that require employers take basic health and safety measures. There is an Act of Parliament governing what the employer must pay as a minimum wage to employees and workers. There are regulations controlling working hours and holiday.

Many of these laws emanated from our membership of the European Union. Directives issued by the European Union have to be transposed into member states' domestic laws within two years.

Many such directives have been issued and member states like the UK have complied with them by passing Acts of Parliament, statutory instruments or regulations. Examples of transposed directives include regulations on employees' rights following a transfer of an undertaking, rules governing what consultation should take place when making 20 or more employees redundant to Acts of Parliament prohibiting many forms of discrimination in the workplace. Article 119 of the founding Treaty of Rome sets out that men and women should be paid equally and have equal pay terms in employment contracts if men and women are doing similar or like work in the same or associated employment.

Despite what feels like a deluge of regulation in the workplace in the last 30 years, there is no statutory definition of bullying. The European Union has not regulated against bullying in the workplace directly. The UK parliament has made no laws specifically defining and outlawing bullying in the workplace. Harassment on the other hand has been defined both at the level of EU directive and within the Equality Act 2010 and the Protection from Harassment Act 1997.

Bullying and harassment as terms are used interchangeably by employees and workers. Harassment is likely to amount to bullying but bullying won't necessarily amount to harassment. Harassment is a sub-set of bullying.

There are statutory definitions of harassment – one contained in the Equality Act 2010 and the other contained in the Protection from Harassment Act 1997. There is a statutory definition of victimisation. Bullying has yet to be defined by statute. That is a surprising omission.

There are some acts that are unlawful in the workplace that are so broadly defined that bullying will fit within the definition. The Employment Rights Act 1996 prevents employees being dismissed or subjected to a detriment if the reason for being subjected to a detriment or dismissed is because the employee:

1. Has made a protected disclosure under the Whistleblowing regime.
2. Has made a disclosure about health and safety concerns.
3. Has refused to work on a Sunday.
4. Has exercised a right under Working Time Regulations.
5. Is a Pension Scheme Trustee.
6. Has made a disclosure about pension auto-enrolment.
7. Is an Employee Representative.
8. Has made a Flexible Working request.
9. Has made a request as a young employee for study or training.
10. Has or is about to exercise a right to family leave.
11. Is a member of a Trade Union.
12. Has applied for Trade Union recognition.
13. Has queried whether being paid national minimum wage.
14. Is a fixed term employee.
15. Has acted as a companion at a disciplinary or grievance hearing.
16. Has or is about to go on jury service.
17. Is on a zero hours contract.

Caselaw has interpreted detriment to mean disadvantage in Ministry of Defence v Jeremiah [1979] IRLR 436. Clearly being bullied in the workplace is a disadvantage or detriment.

However, in order to make a claim under the detriment provisions there has to be a causal link between the detriment suffered, the bullying, and the protected act. That is sometimes difficult as bullies don't need a reason to bully. They just bully as part of their management or supervisory style or as part of their character as individuals.

2.1 Secondary sources: case law, or Codes of Practice that can be taken into account by judicial decision makers

ACAS does not have a Code of Practice on Bullying. ACAS has published a guide for employers and employees on bullying. An Employment Tribunal can take account of a Code of Practice in determining its decision. An Employment Tribunal will also look at ACAS Guides if their attention is drawn to the material.

ACAS definition within "Bullying and Harassment at Work – A Guide for Employees" is as follows:

> "*Offensive, intimidating, malicious, or insulting behaviour, an abuse or misuse of power through means that undermine, humiliate, denigrate or injure the recipient.*"

The examples of bullying given in the guide include:

2.1.1. Spreading malicious rumours.

2.1.2. Copying in others on critical memos or emails.

2.1.3. Insulting someone by word or behaviour.

2.1.4. Ridiculing or demeaning someone.

2.1.5. Exclusion or victimisation.

2.1.6. Unfair treatment.

2.1.7. Overbearing supervision or other misuse of power.

2.1.8. Making threats about job security without foundation.

2.1.9. Deliberately undermining a competent worker by overloading and constant criticism.

2.1.10. Preventing individuals progressing by deliberately blocking opportunities for promotion or training.

The ACAS definition is a workable definition. The examples of bullying behaviour are useful, however it may have been better if the word "deliberately" had not been used at example 2.1.9. A manager could leave a direct report feeling bullied by "overloading and constant criticism" even if the manager's actions were unintentional rather than deliberate. That's bullying behaviour, albeit unintentional. Intent in the law on harassment goes to the gravity of the unlawful act not whether the unlawful act has happened.

So the secondary sources give some definition to what behaviour amounts to bullying but suggests that bullying needs to be intentional to fit within the definition. Some bullying behaviour may not be intentional but may leave the recipient feeling bullied.

The ACAS Code is specifically referred to in the case of alleged ministerial bullying below.

2.2. Case law on Bullying

The second source of definition for bullying is caselaw. The legal system in the UK is described as a common law system. The common law develops as circumstances and societal mores change. It is no surprise therefore that in a common law system much of the guidance on what behaviour should be found as bullying comes from case law.

There have been reported cases on bullying. The cases have not given a definition of bullying but have given some examples of what sorts of behaviour amounts to bullying conduct.

The best-known case is **Horkulak v Cantor Fitzgerald** [2004] **IRLR 942**. In that case the employer's Managing Director, a Mr Amaitis, was found to have subjected the Claimant to bullying behaviour. The findings were as follows:

> *"In my judgment the contract broke down and the position of the claimant became intolerable because Mr Amaitis took every opportunity to vent his disapproval of the claimant, to the claimant and sometimes in the presence of others ... Far from having any discussions and giving advice he uttered intemperate, summary views in foul and abusive language. His solution seems to have been to frighten the claimant into performing according to the standards he required and to make it plain that any contrary view which questioned his authority will not be tolerated."*

Case law provides thin gruel for those looking for a definition of bullying. Examples of behaviour that amounts to bullying are given but not a wider generic definition.

In the case of Spadijier v Montenegro, Article 8 of the Human Rights Act was engaged. Article 8 gives everyone the right to a private life. In this case a prison officer who reported her colleagues for indecent conduct suffered in retaliation the form of being spat at, verbally abused, had her windscreen broken. She was required to make her colleagues coffee.

The ECHR said there was a positive obligation on the State employer to protect staff from bullying retaliation. In this case the Claimant the right to private life breached. The Human Rights Act is only directly enforced against state employers.

In the case of R v Prime Minister and Minister for the Civil Service [2021] EWHC 3279, the court found that inappropriate bullying by a

Minister against a senior civil servant, couldn't breach the ministerial code in certain circumstances. In interpreting the code the court said that intention to bully was not a required component. The court said that bullying must be interpreted objectively. Bullying is bullying if it's offensive, intimidating, malicious or insulting behaviour and that behaviour may fall within that definition even if the perpetrator was unaware it had that effect.

The second hub of bullying was "abuse or misuse of power in ways that undermine, humiliate, denigrate or warning the recipient.

In the case of Diggins v Bar Standards Board [2020] EWHC 467 (Admin) the High Court found that a Barrister's tweet would amount to professional misconduct. Given the toxicity of certain sections in social media. This is a clear warning for professionals to conduct themselves appropriately.

3. Other sources such as academic papers, and the Health and Safety Executive.

The Health and Safety Executive have a paper called "Bullying a review of the literature". In the paper, as its title suggests, the researchers have reviewed the academic literature.

The definition of bullying that the HSE finds has most academic consensus is as follows:

> *"Bullying at work means harassing, offending, socially excluding someone or negatively affecting someone's work tasks. In order for the label bullying (or mobbing) to be applied to a particular activity, interaction or process, it has to occur repeatedly and regularly (e.g., weekly) and over a period of time (e.g. about six months). Bullying is an escalating process in the course of which the person confronted ends up in an inferior position and becomes the target of systematic negative social acts. A conflict cannot be called bullying if the incident is an*

isolated event or if two parties of approximately equal 'strength' are in conflict"

However there is not agreement amongst academics on that definition and the following issues are subject to debate:

- Does the bullying have to be intentional?
- Does there have to be repetition or is once enough?
- Can bullying become institutional rather than individual?
- Does there have to be an inequality of power or position?

A review of the all the sources shows that there is no consensus amongst the academics on a definition of bullying, no statutory definition by the law makers and very little definition given by the Judges in cases that come before them. The Courts have left it to the good sense of the Judge to find bullying where the facts and context permit without being too prescriptive about a definition.

4. What legal rights does an employee have not to be bullied in the workplace?

The ACAS guide makes clear that unlike harassment which is actionable as a freestanding legal claim under discrete sections of legislation, an employee cannot make a freestanding complaint of bullying to either an Employment Tribunal or the High Court. Bullying is actionable as a legal claim, but the legal claim usually comes under another heading. The route into a legal claim of bullying is signposted as a different sort of claim.

So in order to bring a legal claim where bullying is the main allegation how is the claim framed legally? What legal rights are being enforced?

Not to be bullied in the workplace is a negative right. The positive right is to be treated with respect.

Employee's legal rights can usually be found in three places:

- The contract of employment (including implied terms).

- The Employer's legal responsibilities owed to employees including the duty of care.

- The statutory rights Parliament has given to employees.

For the sake of ease we will look at these sources of rights and duties separately. In practice, however, the distinctions overlap.

An employer's legal responsibility to provide a safe place of work can become an implied contractual right for an employee. Similarly an employee's statutory rights can become, in certain circumstances, implied into the contract.

The distinction is perhaps more useful when we look at the methods and mechanisms available to an employee for enforcing their contractual or statutory rights or alleging an employer has breached a legal responsibility which it owes the employee.

5. Bullying at work – the contractual position

We will look at contractual rights first. When looking at rights under the contract, we need to differentiate between the right itself and the method of enforcement. More often than not the method of enforcing a contractual right is via a statutory right. Whilst we have separated out contractual rights from statutory rights the method of enforcing those rights shows that there is plenty of overlap.

An employee's contract is made up of terms and conditions of employment. There is a legal obligation on employers to give an employee a written statement of terms and conditions within two months of starting employment (set to become on or before the first day of Employment from April 2020).

The contract of employment has the following sorts of terms:

(a) Express Terms – these terms that are either written down or expressly agreed. It is unlikely that the contract of employment or the statement of terms and conditions will say in black and white, in written down form, that the employee has the contractual right not to be bullied.

(b) Incorporated terms – those terms are written down in another document outside the contract of employment or statement of terms and condition but are incorporated into the contract by reference. It is possible that an employee handbook or policy and procedure may give the employee the contractual right to a workplace that is dignified and free from bullying or harassment. That handbook or policy and procedure can become contractual if it is expressed as contractual or has become contractual through custom and practice.

(c) An employer may have a handbook or policies within a handbook that set out rules and requirements about behaviour at work, dignity at work or bullying and harassment in the workplace. Whether a policy or all or part of a handbook has become contractual is fact sensitive.

In the case of **Keeley v Fosroc International Limited** [2006] **IRLR 961** a document outside the employment contract, a handbook, became incorporated into the contract and became contractual by incorporation but also by implication. Factors that led to the handbook becoming incorporated were:

"The handbook was explicitly referred to in the employee's terms and conditions of employment. The language of the handbook in particular the part on enhanced redundancy payments was the language of contractual entitlement. The section used the word entitled."

There have been other cases though which have not incorporated policies or other documents governing the workplace into the contract.

In **Dryden v Greater Glasgow Health Board** [1992] **IRLR 469** works rules were found to have no contractual effect.

Similarly in **Grant v South West Trains Limited** [1998] **IRLR 188 the Tribunal** found that an Equal Opportunities Policy had no contractual effect.

It is possible that an employer has a handbook that gives an employee the contractual right not to be bullied, but it won't be commonplace. Most handbooks, policies and procedures are aspirational rather than binding obligations.

Workers in a workplace may have a contract for services or consultancy agreement. Those documents may reference abiding by the Handbook or specific policies and procedures, in which case workers may have similar incorporated terms not to work in a workplace that allows bullying.

(d) Implied terms – these terms aren't written down but are implied into the contract to give the contract business efficacy or the terms are implied by custom and practice. Within every employee's contract will be implied terms. The most common implied term is the term of trust and confidence.

The term of Trust and Confidence is set out in the case of **Malik v BCCI** [1997] **IRLR 462**. The term of trust and confidence implied into every contract of employment means that employers shall not:

> *"without reasonable and proper cause, conduct itself in a manner calculated or likely to destroy or seriously damage the relationship of confidence and trust between employer and employee."*

Bullying behaviour will usually amount to a breach of trust and confidence as will allowing bullying behaviour in the workplace.

There have been plenty of cases involving allegations of a breach of the implied term of trust and confidence or the implied right to work in a healthy and safe workplace.

Principles extracted from these cases which may have some relevance to bullying cases are as follows:

British Broadcasting Corporation v Beckett [1983] **IRLR** 43

The imposition of a disciplinary penalty that was grossly out of proportion to the disciplinary offence can amount to a breach of the implied term. Further the intention of the manager applying the penalty is not relevant. The manager may believe in good faith that he or she has the power under the disciplinary procedure to impose the penalty. However that intention does not:

> *"derogate from the general proposition that a party to the contract may so act that his conduct if viewed* ***objectively*** *amounts to a fundamental breach of his contractual obligations."*

So a court or an Employment Tribunal will look objectively at whether an allegation of bullying breaches the implied term of trust and confidence.

The intention of the perpetrator will not determine whether the conduct repudiates the contract. This therefore removes the requirement for the perpetrator of the bullying to have intended his behaviour to have that effect. The question becomes has the behaviour, when viewed objectively, left the employee feeling bullied. As we shall see later that test is similar to the test of harassment on proscribed grounds.

Waltons & Morse v Dorrington [1997] **IRLR 488**

This case involved a secretary having to work in an office where her colleagues smoked. The secretary eventually resigned and claimed constructive dismissal. The EAT held that it was an implied term of the contract that:

> "*the employer will provide and monitor for employees, as far as is reasonably practicable, a working environment which is reasonably suitable for the performance by them of their contractual duties.*"

The starting point for the implication of such a term is the duty of an employer under section 2 (2) of the Health and Safety at Work Act:

> "*to provide and maintain a working environment for employees that is reasonably safe and without risk to health and is adequate as regards facilities and arrangements for their welfare at work.*"

An Employment Tribunal can look at whether actions and behaviours of the employer pose a risk to the health and safety and welfare of the employees. They can look at the duty of care owed to the employee to see whether that duty of care has been observed or not.

Graham Oxley Tool Steels Limited v Firth [1980] IRLR 135

In this case an employer was held to be in breach of the implied term that the employee should be furnished with a working environment which is suitable to enable him or her to perform his or her obligations under the contract. In that case the working environment was so cold that the employee terminated her contract of employment

> *"owing to freezing working conditions which I have to work in."*

Hilton Hotels (UK) Limited v Protopapa [1990] IRLR 316

In this case a manager's conduct in reprimanding an employee in front of other employees for making a dental appointment without first asking permission was:

> *"officious and insensitive"* and left the employee *"humiliated, intimidated, and degraded to such an extent that there was a breach of trust and confidence which went to the root of the contract."*

In that case the incident was a one off. However both the Employment Tribunal and Employment Appeal Tribunal saw that one incident was enough. Furthermore, whilst bullying was not specifically alleged the behaviour of a manager publicly criticising a report does fall within the ACAS example of bullying behaviour in the Guidance.

Palamanor Limited trading as Chaplins Night Club v Cedron [1978] IRLR 303

In this case an employee was questioned by the manager of the club why he was late. The employee denied he was late. The manager then insulted him by saying:

> *"You are a big bastard, a big cunt, you are pig headed, you think you are always right." When the employee said the manager had no right to talk to him like that, the manager replied that "I can talk to you any way I like, you big cunt…if you don't like it you can go…If you leave me now, don't bother to collect your money, papers or anything else. I'll make sure you don't get a job anywhere in London."*

Both the employment tribunal and employment appeal tribunal concluded that one incident was enough, the intention of the perpetrator was not material and common sense should be adopted in determining whether the incident was sufficiently serious to repudiate the contract as a breach of the implied term of trust and confidence.

Morrow v Safeway Stores PLC [2002] IRLR 9

In Morrow the employee was reprimanded in front of colleagues and a customer by her manager.

The employee resigned in a state of distress. The Employment Appeal Tribunal held that the

> *"Employment Tribunal had led itself into error by seeking to separate out the actual words spoken, which it thought were not in themselves unreasonable, from the circumstances in which the reprimand took place."*

Context is therefore important in determining whether conduct or behaviour is sufficiently serious to repudiate the contract.

Wigan Borough Council v Davies [1979] IRLR 127

The employer, Wigan Borough Council, promised an employee orally following a complaint that they would offer all reasonable support to enable her to work in the workplace free from harassment and without disruption from other members of staff. Her colleagues subsequently sent the employee to Coventry and the employee resigned claiming breach of contract.

The Employment Tribunal and the Employment Appeal Tribunal found that the agreement reached orally with her employer that they would offer all reasonable support was an express term. Furthermore, there was an implied term to that effect anyway. A breach of that term entitled the employee to walk out and claim constructive dismissal.

Walker v Northumberland County Council [1995] **IRLR 35**

In this case a manager of a social work team had a nervous breakdown. Mr Walker was responsible for a high-volume caseload, some of which involved child abuse cases. On his return to work the Council failed to follow up on agreed actions. Mr Walker then went off sick again, never to return.

The Court held that it was not reasonably foreseeable for the employer to foresee that Mr Walker was at risk of a nervous breakdown prior to his first absence. It was however reasonably foreseeable on his return and the employer had failed in its duty of care towards its employee.

In particular the Court held that:

> *"There has been little judicial authority on the extent to which an employer owes to his employees a duty not to cause them psychiatric damage by the volume or character of the work which the employees are required to perform. It is clear law that an employer has a duty to provide his employee with a reasonably safe system of work and to take reasonable steps to protect him from risks which are reasonably foreseeable."*

This was then qualified by the following:

> *"That said, the duty of an employer public body, whether in contract or tort, to provide a safe system of work is, as I have said, a duty only to do what is reasonable..."*

WA Goold (Pearmak) Limited v McConnell [1995[**IRLR 516**

There is an implied term in a contract of employment that the employers will reasonably and promptly afford a reasonable opportunity to their employees to obtain redress of any grievance.

Summary

An employee has the following implied contractual rights:

- The right for their employer not to act in a way calculated or likely to destroy trust and confidence. Bullying words or behaviour can be a breach of trust and confidence depending on the circumstances. The intent of the perpetrator is not relevant. The test is objective.

- The right to have a working environment provided and monitored for employees, as far as is reasonably practicable, which is reasonably suitable for the performance by them of their contractual duties.

- The right to have the employer offer all reasonable support to enable the employee to work in the workplace free from harassment and without disruption from other members of staff.

- The right to have a safe place of work.

- The right to appropriate support.

An employee may have the following express contractual rights:

- A handbook or policy and procedure that is contractual. Within that handbook or policy and procedure an express contractual right that an employee or worker is entitled to a workplace that is free from harassment or bullying. Most such documents are stated to be non-contractual so it will be relatively rare for an employee or worker to have an express contractual right not to be bullied.

6. Bullying at Work – the statutory position

The key statutory right for most people in the workplace is the statutory right not to be unfairly dismissed.

In order to qualify for the right, you have to:

1. Be an employee.
2. Have two years' service.
3. Be dismissed.

There are some exceptions to the two-year service rule, namely if an employee is dismissed for raising a statutory right-for example the employee has made a public interest disclosure, made a request for flexible working, or asserted a statutory right.

It is the final part of the definition that will lead to many claims being made for bullying.

Dismissal has three meanings under the Employment Rights Act 1996:

1. Dismissal with or without notice by the employer.
2. Expiry of a fixed term contract without it being renewed.

3. The employee resigns in circumstances where the employee is entitled to treat the contract as terminated.

It is this latter type of dismissal which will lead to Employment Tribunal claims for unfair dismissal on grounds of bullying. Very few employees will be dismissed by their employer for being bullied. Likewise very few employees will not have a contract renewed because they have been bullied. It is the third type of dismissal that will be the refuge for many employees who have been bullied. The third type of dismissal is known by the shorthand of constructive dismissal. In order to claim constructive dismissal, following the case of Western Excavators v Sharp, the employee has to jump over four hurdles. If they knock any of the hurdles over then their claim for dismissal will fail. The hurdles are:

1. That a term of their contract has been breached.

2. That the breach is a repudiatory one, that is sufficiently serious to entitle the employee to walk out.

3. That the employee has resigned because of the breach.

4. That the employee has not delayed their resignation for too long.

If an employee is being bullied in the workplace either by their manager or supervisor or by their colleagues, it is open for the employee to walk out by resigning and claiming constructive dismissal. The resignation can be with or without notice.

A constructive dismissal is the mirror opposite of a gross misconduct dismissal. In a gross misconduct dismissal the employer is dismissing the employee without notice for committing an act of gross misconduct. An act of gross misconduct is a repudiatory breach of contract by the employee. Examples include theft, fighting, and fiddled expenses.

In a constructive dismissal claim the employee is alleging that the employer has committed a repudiatory breach of contract entitling the employee to accept the breach by resignation. In summary the employee is claiming that the employer has committed an act of gross misconduct.

Many employers have a disciplinary procedure. In most disciplinary procedures bullying is listed as an act of gross misconduct. Indeed the ACAS Code of Practice in its appendix has a model disciplinary procedure which cites as an example of gross misconduct "bullying or harassment."

Therefore if an employee is being bullied he or she can treat that bullying as a repudiation of the contract and resign. If repudiation is proved then the claim for unfair dismissal will succeed.

As we have seen in the above cases unreasonable and overbearing conduct by an employer, through their management team, can amount to a breach of an implied term of trust and confidence. A breach of the implied term of trust and confidence is a repudiatory breach – Nary v Archbishop of Westminster.

One point of contention is whether an employee has to lodge a grievance before resigning? The short answer is no but a failure to lodge a grievance can undermine the credibility of the claim as many employers adopt the position that if an employee has not formally complained about an issue the issue hasn't happened. Similarly the employer can argue that had a grievance been lodged the issue could have been nipped in the bud.

An Employment Tribunal takes a more nuanced approach, recognising that employees have practical difficulties in raising a grievance, particularly if management are implicated in the bullying.

So if an employer allows an employee to be bullied in the workplace that can give rise to a constructive unfair dismissal claim. Constructive dismissal claims require the employee to take action. That action is resignation which cites that the bullying is the reason for the resignation.

So an act of bullying or a failure to prevent bullying can give rise to a constructive dismissal claim. However constructive dismissal claims have a cap on the financial award of a year's pay or £115,115 whichever is the lower. The £115,115 cap is the cap in 2024–2025 and is uprated in April each year.

The cap may therefore inadequately compensate for the loss suffered, particularly if the loss is a loss of career or damage to mental or physical health that curtails earning ability.

Where health has been impacted an employee may want to consider a claim for negligence against the employer. Whilst negligence claims are common law claims, relying on the concept of a duty of care owed by the employer to the employee, health and safety law has codified much of the employer's duty of care.

An employer has to have employers' liability insurance. An employer has to abide by the laws relating to health and safety in the workplace.

What are those laws?

The common law of negligence. In order to prove negligence an employee or worker has to show the following:

1. The employer owes them a duty of care.

2. The employer has failed to take a step which can be reasonably expected in the circumstances. The employer has breached the duty of care.

3. Such a breach was negligent.

4. Damage suffered as a result of that failure.

In cases of bullying and harassment the personal injury that arises from the negligence is usually psychiatric injury.

The keynote case on stress at work which sets out the parameters of the employer's duty of care is Sutherland v Hatton [2002] IRLR 263. In that case the Court of Appeal in the lead judgement given by Lady Hale noted that:

> *First, and perhaps contrary to popular belief, harmful levels of stress are most likely to occur in situations where people feel powerless or trapped. These are more likely to affect people on the shop floor or at the more junior levels than those who are in a position to shape what they do. Second, stress – in the sense of a perceived mismatch between the pressures of the job and the individual's ability to meet them – is a psychological phenomenon, but it can lead to either physical or mental ill health or both. When considering the issues raised by these four cases, in which the claimants all suffered psychiatric illnesses, it may therefore be important to bear in mind that the same issues might arise had they instead suffered some stress-related physical disorder, such as ulcers, heart disease or hypertension.*

Lady Hale also took us back to first principles:

> *Liability in negligence depends upon three interrelated requirements: the existence of a duty to take care; a failure to take the care which can reasonably be expected in the circumstances; and damage suffered as a result of that failure.*

She said the following about foreseeability:

> *Whichever is the correct analysis, the threshold question is whether this kind of harm to this particular employee was reasonably foreseeable. The question is not whether psychiatric injury is foreseeable in a person of 'ordinary fortitude'. The employer's duty is owed to each individual employee, not to some as yet unidentified outsider*

She noted that a particularly important feature of any claim will be the signs emanating from the employee. And whilst every case will be different it should be reasonably obvious when an employer has to take action:

> *In view of the many difficulties of knowing when and why a particular person will go over the edge from pressure to stress and from stress to injury to health, the indications must be plain enough for any reasonable employer to realise that he should do something about it.*

Once it is established that harm is reasonably foreseeable the employer must then act with a duty of care. Lady hale stated:

> *the employer can only reasonably be expected to take steps which are likely to do some good.*

A claim for damages for bullying will have the following framework:

1. An employer owes a duty of care to employees and workers to have a safe workplace.

2. Bullying and harm from bullying is reasonably foreseeable.

3. An employer should take steps to prevent bullying and its harmful effects.

4. An employer may and will be liable for losses caused by bullying, in particular damage to health.

Cases alleging negligence involving Bullying:

There have been a number of high-profile cases involving allegations of bullying where the employee has suffered ill health and the employer is sued for damages for negligence for the loss of health and the loss of income arising.

Perhaps the best-known case is **Green v. DB Group Services (UK) Ltd [2006] EWHC 1898** (QB) where a Ms Green went to work in the Company Secretarial department of Deutsche Bank. During the selection process DB became aware of the fact that Ms Green had had a traumatic childhood involving abuse from a family member and that she had suffered from stress and depression as a result.

Whilst at DB Ms Green suffered bullying at the hands of 4 female colleagues who had a history of bullying others in the department. The bullying consisted of freezing Ms Green out, laughing at her, hiding her mail, having loud conversations near her desk whilst she wa son the phone. HR did not intervene despite a complaint to them.

Subsequently the Claimant was bullied by a male manager in the department and she eventually ended up breaking down and needing hospital treatment.

She subsequently sued DB for negligence and under the Protection from Harassment Act 1997.

The High Court framed the issues to be determined as follows regarding the negligence case:

> *Has the claimant established that the conduct complained of took place and, if so, did it amount to bullying or harassment in the ordinary connotation of those terms? In addressing this question, it is the cumulative effect of the conduct which has to be considered rather than the individual incidents relied on. (ii) Did those involved in the victimisation or bullying know, or ought they reasonably to have known, that their conduct might cause the claimant harm? (iii) By the exercise of reasonable care, could they have taken steps which would have avoided that harm? (iv) Were their actions so connected with their employment as to render the defendants vicariously liable for them?*

The Court found in favour of Ms Green and awarded her substantial 6 figure damages.

Because having a safe workplace is a legal obligation an employee who complains of bullying by way of a grievance may also be making a public interest disclosure and have protection because of that.

The public interest disclosure regime, or whistleblowing to give the more usual moniker, allows an employee or worker to make a complaint to the employer by supplying information to the employer that they are failing in their legal obligation of having a safe workplace by allowing bullying in it.

In order to qualify as a public interest disclosure the employee will have to show that he or she believes it is in the public interest to raise the matter. That may not be too difficult as either the employee or worker can show that there is a pattern or culture of bullying that affects a number of people in which case that ought to qualify as a public interest disclosure following the Chesterton case.

Alternatively the employee's grievance may qualify as a public interest disclosure if he or she reasonably believes that the effects of bullying, increased ill health and absence, does have a public interest angle in terms of its impact on the wider economy through productivity losses and increased use of the National Health Service.

In summary therefore the legal position on bullying has not been compartmentalised as a separate legal claim.

Claims of bullying are usually brought in one of two ways:

1. By way of a claim in Employment Tribunal.

    a) This will normally be a claim for unfair dismissal claim in the employment tribunal. The right not to be unfairly dismissed is a statutory right.

        (1) An early conciliation certificate will need to be obtained from ACAS within 3 months of the effective date of

termination and a claim lodged with the Employment Tribunal within 1 month of the date of the early conciliation certificate.

(2) In most cases the dismissal will be constructive, the employee will have resigned in response to an act of bullying that repudiates the contract.

(3) The repudiation will usually be of the implied term of trust and confidence unless there is an express right in the contract not to be bullied.

(4) Sometimes a dismissal by an employer may be an act of bullying.

(5) Unfair dismissal compensation is capped at a year's pay or £115,115 whatever is the lower, together with a basic award which is calculated in exactly the same way as a statutory redundancy payment.

b) If an employee brings a grievance that alleges bullying that grievance may be treated as a public interest disclosure.

c) If the employee is subsequently dismissed or suffers a detriment for making the disclosure the employee can bring a claim in the Employment Tribunal.

d) The time limits noted above will apply.

e) However public interest claims have two notable features, firstly since the Osipov case a claim can be brought against the individual employee or worker who subjects the employee to a detriment, including dismissal, because they have brought the grievance.

f) Secondly awards of compensation for public interest cases are uncapped.

2. Alternatively a claim can be brought in the civil courts – County Court or High Court. This claim will be one of damages arising from either a breach of a duty of care or a breach of a contractual term, normally the former. Damages claims are uncapped. The employee will have to prove the following:

    a) That the employer owed them a duty of care not to be bullied in the workplace.

    b) That duty has been breached.

    c) It was reasonably foreseeable that a breach would result in loss.

    d) The loss was caused by the breach.

Another way of looking at it as an employer is that allowing a workplace to have a bullying culture is a health and safety issue. Most employers take health and safety very seriously. For example, as part of induction many employees will be inducted into health and safety measures the employer has in place in particular the need to wear personal protection equipment like hard hats in certain areas. A failure to adhere to health and safety processes is often treated as gross misconduct by employers in their disciplinary procedures. Many employers now have a mental health first aider.

Bullying which can cause stress and affect mental health should be treated no differently as a health risk and employers should have risk assessments in place and should take risk prevention and mitigations measures. Let's not forget the people behind the cases. Here is their story.

SB is a client – here's her story of bullying at work which resulted in her boss spray painting 'bitch' on her car:

"Will today be the day your life changes forever? Will today be the day that you attract the eye of a stranger? Will someone you have known for years develop an unhealthy obsession with you? I cannot tell you at what exact point

my life changed. And you probably wouldn't be able to tell anyone else when evil came into your life. Rather than a crash, mine was more like a slow drip. A series of episodes that on their own seemed upsetting and frustrating rather than something that has made me question how my life would end and re-write my will, and make my loved ones aware of end of life wishes."

Does that seem a little dramatic? Perhaps, until you have been on the receiving end of something so deliberate. Stalking is referred to as murder in slow motion by some of the experts.

This is something I never wanted to write, and I hope you never need, but I wish there was a self-help guide for Victims of Stalking when I needed one. There is support out there, but it took me hours of research to find information. I want to demonstrate to everyone that you do not have to have received a great education, you don't have to be a celebrity, you don't have to be young or gorgeous, and you don't have to be rich to attract the eye of a stalker. And you don't have to have or be any of those things to fight back.

CHAPTER TWO

HARASSMENT IN THE WORKPLACE

In this chapter we will look at how harassment on one of the prescribed grounds became unlawful in the workplace.

How the Framework was built

The term harassment has an interesting back story. It became a term with a statutorily defined meaning following the passage of an EU directive and finally became consolidated in the 2010 Equality Act.

Prior to that harassment was a term that developed through cases brought under the separate pieces of discrimination legislation. We can track its development by looking back at the legislation and subsequent case law.

The EU's Role

When the UK joined the European Economic Community in 1973, signing the Treaty of Rome, the UK committed to passing into law EEC directives. As the EEC became the EC and then the EU its area of competence over member states' law incrementally increased much to the chagrin of Eurosceptics in the UK who saw ceding sovereignty over a limited number of areas as emasculating parliament in the UK.

The EEC and the EU are founded on four pillars: freedom of movement of capital, freedom of movement of people, freedom of movement of services, and freedom of movement of goods within the EU single market. The EU single market seeks to remove friction that may deter the freedoms being exercised. Having a common framework of minimum employment rights goes some way to ensuring citizens in EU member states can exercise their rights.

There is a legal framework in place within the EU. That framework develops law within the European Commission. Legislative proposals coming out of the European Commission are then scrutinised, reviewed and revised in the EU parliament. The EU parliament then passes the law. That law, called a directive, has to be implemented within the member states of the EU within two years. A failure to implement a directive either at all or in full will result in infraction proceedings taken by the EU against the member state.

Furthermore, each right that is enshrined into member state law has to have an effective remedy for infringement of that right as well as be enforceable as a right. Sitting atop of the judicial hierarchy for determining cases involving law developed in the EU as a directive is the European Court of Justice.

As you will see the European Court of Justice has taken a proactive approach in determining whether a member state's national law has complied with the underlying EU directive.

The ECJ interprets EU law in a purposive way. That means the ECJ judges try to give effect to the purpose of the law when determining the meaning of a directive and in arriving at a judgment. That purposive approach to judicial decision-making runs counter to the UK's jurisprudential approach which is for UK judges to adopt a literal approach to interpreting what words in a statute mean. The UK's approach is to determine what the words on the page mean, the ECJ's approach is to give purpose to the writers of the law's intent in drafting it. UK courts, in cases involving laws implemented from EU directives now adopt a purposive approach to interpretation.

In theory there should be regulatory alignment within the EU member states as well as regulatory alignment for goods and services sold within the EU but manufactured outside the EU. Electrical goods sold within the single market, for example, have to conform to EU wide regulation of electrical safety and each electrical good in the EU single market has to be certified as meeting the EU standard – that is done by way of a system of product quality control which is then assured by way of testing and certified as EU compliant by sticking a small CE certificate on the good.

Similarly, as EU citizens have the right to move within the single market and take up employment in any member state, the EU has in place a common framework of laws that apply across the workplaces situated anywhere within the EU.

The framework is very much a floor rather than a ceiling. Member states have to legislate at a minimum at the floor but can copper bottom the EU minimum.

The EU minimum for the number of days holiday, for example, within the EU is 20 days. The UK has improved on the ground floor right by providing for full time employees and workers to have a minimum of 28 days paid holiday per year, or a pro-rata amount if the employment is part time.

Within the founding Treaty of Rome is Article 119 which provides that there should be no pay disparity for men and women doing equal work in the EEC, now EU. On joining the EEC in 1973 the UK passed the Equal Pay Act 1970 which provided for women to have an implied equal pay clause in their contract of employment if women were doing work that was of equal value, or equal rating or similar to comparable men's work in the employer's organisation.

Likewise, in the 1970s the UK passed the Sex Discrimination Act which came into force in 1975 which outlawed discrimination in the workplace based on gender or marital status.

The Race Relations Act was passed in 1976 which outlawed discrimination in the workplace based on race.

The Disability Discrimination Act came into force in 1995. It gave disabled employees positive rights in the workplace as well as imposing obligations on the employer to adjust the workplace to accommodate a disabled employee or a disabled prospective employee.

The prohibition on sex discrimination in the workplace is common throughout each EU member state's statute book.

The Sex Discrimination Act 1975

In the UK the Sex Discrimination Act defined three principal types of discrimination:

1. Direct discrimination which is where an individual treats an employee or worker to less favourable treatment on grounds of sex during employment or at the recruitment stage.

2. Indirect discrimination is imposing a requirement or condition which on the face of it is gender neutral but fewer of one sex can comply with the condition or requirement. The condition or requirement will not be indirectly discriminatory if the employer can justify the condition or requirement. In seeking to justify a condition or requirement the impact on the employee or worker who is unable to comply with it is weighed up against the organisational need to have the condition or requirement. For example, the requirement to be 5 foot 8 to join the police impacts disproportionately on women and could not be justified.

3. Victimisation which is treating someone less favourably because they have done a protected act. A protected act is defined as a complaint of discrimination or giving information or evidence about alleged discrimination either internally or externally in a legal case.

The Sex Discrimination Act covered discrimination on grounds of sex and marital status. The Sex Discrimination Act defines what discrimination is in broad and generic terms and then specifies what acts are unlawful in the workplace. The Act outlaws discrimination, as defined against employees, workers and applicants for employment.

The Act makes it unlawful for an individual to discriminate in one of the ways defined:

- At the recruitment stage.
- In the terms and conditions and benefits offered during employment.
- In the access to training and promotion.
- At dismissal.
- And at any time during employment being "subjected to a detriment."

The legislation is framed to impose a liability on the employee or worker who discriminates in one of the ways defined. The Act also makes the employer vicariously liable for unlawful acts committed by their employees or workers during employment.

ECJ's role in shaping the framework

Up until the mid-1990s the Sex Discrimination Act had a cap on compensation. That cap was identical to the then cap on unfair dismissal compensation which was then approximately £12,000.00.

A case was referred to the European Court of Justice to determine whether the cap on compensation gave full effect to the Equal Treatment

Directive. The ECJ determined that it did not. The UK had to remove the cap.

Similarly the Sex Discrimination Act exempted some employers from its provisions, in particular the Armed Forces. However that exemption was referred to the ECJ and again the exemption was lifted so that Armed Forces personnel came within the ambit of the Act.

One of the first beneficiaries of the removal of this exemption was service personnel who were dismissed from their Armed Forces service when they became pregnant. The Armed Forces, because they were previously exempt from the Sex Discrimination Act, had the contractual right to terminate any female employee in the services when they became pregnant.

I acted for many service personnel in the mid-1990s who claimed compensation for loss of career for their dismissals. Those dismissals for pregnancy were unlawful and had always been unlawful since the day the Sex Discrimination Act was passed as the directive did not permit such an exemption.

A public sector employee or worker can rely on the underlying EU directive rather than the domestic law. That right circumvents any member state as an employer from giving themselves an exemption from EU directives. As the underlying Equal Treatment Directive had no exemption for personnel employed by a member state's armed forces then a member of the UK Armed Forces could rely on the EU directive rather than the defective national legislation, the Sex Discrimination Act.

The Race Relations Act 1976 and the Disability Discrimination Act 1995

The Race Relations Act and the Disability Discrimination Act shared a similar framework as the Sex Discrimination Act 1975 in defining discrimination, in outlining what acts were unlawful and in imposing liability on both the perpetrator and their employer.

The Disability Discrimination Act defined disability to cover those with long term physical and medical impairments which, ignoring the effects of medication, substantially impaired that person's ability to carry out day to day activities. Long term was defined as lasting a year or expected to last a year or the rest of the person's life. Day to day activities was defined by way of statutory guidance to include such everyday activities as carrying a tray, carrying shopping, driving and so on.

The definition of direct discrimination in the Disability Discrimination Act was tweaked in that it permitted employers to justify any act of direct discrimination against disabled employees. Furthermore, it allowed for positive discrimination in favour of disabled employees and gave no right of redress to employees who were not disabled. It imposed requirements on employers to make reasonable adjustments to the workplace to accommodate employees and workers who have a disability.

Race was given a broad definition in the Race Relations Act to cover colour, ethnic origins, national origins, nationality and in so far as a religion had a particular ethnicity on religious grounds as well.

So we can see that discrimination law up until 2010 was developed because of our membership of the EC. We can see the definition of discrimination, the unlawful acts and the way that liability is imposed on individual discriminators as well as their employer. We can also see the ECJ taking a purposive approach in determining that a cap on compensatory awards for discrimination did not give the employee or worker who suffered an unlawful act of discrimination in the workplace adequate redress to enforce their rights.

How did Harassment become an Unlawful Act?

What we cannot see in any of the domestic legislation is any definition of harassment. How the law developed was to make any claim for harassment a claim of direct discrimination. The doorway for a harassment claim was via the direct discrimination route.

The employee or worker had to prove that he or she had been subject to less favourable treatment on grounds of sex or racial grounds, if brought under the Race Relations Act, during employment

The Claimant had to prove that the treatment was less favourable than an actual or hypothetical male comparator in the same or similar circumstances. What that meant was in order to prove a claim of harassment a comparison was inevitable as the claim was a claim of less favourable treatment on grounds of race or sex.

In cases of direct discrimination the courts have adopted a "but for" test to determine whether or not the treatment was on grounds of sex or race.

The question to be posed in claims of alleged direct sex or race discrimination was "*But for the individual's sex or race, would he or she have been treated in that way?*" Asking that question gives a yes or no answer.

In arriving at that yes or no answer the tribunal or court can ignore the intent of the discriminator.

In **James v Eastleigh Borough Council** the Council used the pensionable age as the age at which a Council leisure pass could be issued to residents in the Council's geographic area.

At the time of the case, the mid-1990s, women received their state pension at the age of 60 and men received it at the age of 65.

Whilst the pensionable age condition was on the face of it gender neutral, after applying the but for test it is clear the men were less favourably treated than the women in having to wait an additional five years before being issued with a leisure pass from the Council.

The case went to the House of Lords who found in favour of the male claimant. The reasoning was as follows:

> *"It would not have availed the Birmingham City Council to say that the condition for grammar school entry was to have passed the entrance examination because the pass mark was set at different levels for boys and girls and discriminated against girls on the ground of their sex. By precise parity of reasoning it does not avail the council in this case to say that the condition for free admission to the swimming pool is to have attained pensionable age because pensionable age is set at different levels for men and women and discriminates against men on the ground of their sex. Similarly the subjective reason for the differential treatment in both cases is quite irrelevant. The Birmingham City Council had the best of motives for discriminating as they did. They could not otherwise have matched the entry of boys and girls to the grammar school places available. The council in this case had the best of motives for discriminating as they did. They wished to benefit "those whose resources were likely to have been reduced by retirement" and "to aid the needy, whether male or female." The criterion of pensionable age was a convenient one to apply because it was readily verified by possession of a pension book or a bus pass. But the purity of the discriminator's subjective motive, intention or reason for discriminating cannot save the criterion applied from the objective taint of discrimination on the ground of sex."*

Whilst there was no intent by the Council to treat the residents less favourably on grounds of sex, the Council's intent was to treat all residents the same and equally based on the state pension age, the effect of the rule was to leave men aged 60 to 64 in the Council's geographic area less favourably treated on grounds of sex when compared with women aged 60 to 64, despite the fact that the intent of the Council was benign in that it wished to assist those residents in its geographic area whose only income was the state pension.

So in determining whether less favourable treatment has happened a court or tribunal can look at the effect of the treatment and ask whether but for the recipient's gender would the treatment have happened in similar circumstances.

The courts or tribunals can also ask whether the Claimant's sex was a factor in the decision. Whilst the Council had acted gender neutrally in having the pensionable age condition for receipt of a free leisure pass, pensionable age was, after all, a defined term in the 1976 Social Security Act and a recognised threshold, the treatment was discriminatory as the condition treated men and women aged 60 to 64 differentially with men being less favourably treated in comparison to women.

The fact that the pensionable age definition differentiated between men and women meant that sex did taint the decision of the Council, albeit unintentionally. A court or tribunal can and should ask whether considerations of gender taint the decision-making process.

Sex or gender need not be uppermost in the mind of the decision maker just a brick in the overall decision wall. The intent of the decision maker is irrelevant in answering the question whether the treatment was less favourable on grounds of sex or race. Discrimination happens and like the road to hell can happen with the best of intentions.

How did harassment fit into Direct Discrimination?

One of the first claims of harassment was brought by a Mrs Porcelli against her employer, Strathclyde Regional Council.

Mrs Porcelli was subject to comments and actions which had a sexual and sexist under-current. She eventually transferred to another department within the Council to escape the behaviour. The Employment Tribunal found at first instance that the behaviour was not sex discrimination as the perpetrators would have treated a man that way and furthermore that the treatment was not because of Mrs Porcelli's gender but because the perpetrators disliked her.

The case was appealed and eventually went to the Court of Session. The Court found that the behaviour was discriminatory on grounds of sex and amounted to a detriment, which means no more than a disadvantage. The court held:

> *S.1(1)(a) is concerned with 'treatment' and not with the motive or objective of the person responsible for it. Although in some cases it will be obvious that there is a sex related purpose in the mind of a person who indulges in unwanted and objectionable sexual overtures to a woman or exposes her to offensive sexual jokes or observations that is not this case. But it does not follow that because the campaign pursued against Mrs Porcelli as a whole had no sex related motive or objective, the treatment of Mrs Porcelli by Coles, which was of the nature of 'sexual harassment' is not to be regarded as having been 'on the ground of her sex' within the meaning of s.1(1)(a). In my opinion this particular part of the campaign was plainly adopted against Mrs Porcelli because she was a woman. It was a particular kind of weapon, based upon the sex of the victim, which, as the Industrial Tribunal recognised would not have been used against an equally disliked man. Indeed, I do not understand from the reasons of the Industrial Tribunal that they were not entirely satisfied upon that matter, and they were in my opinion well entitled to be so satisfied upon a proper interpretation of s.1(1)(a).*

In the early cases of claims of sexual harassment involving alleged unlawful acts with a sexual motive or racist intent then any comparison was easy to overcome as the recipient's sex or race motivated the alleged act.

In cases of alleged sexist or racist comments or alleged sexist or racist acts, which did not have any underlying sexual or racist motive, the comparison did come more into play as the alleged perpetrator often ran the defence that any employee or worker, regardless of gender, would have been treated in the same way. Or as it became known "the bastard's defence", the alleged perpetrator was an absolute bastard to all employees or workers and did not differentiate on grounds of gender or race. In order to counter that difficulty the caselaw adopted a more subjective approach in determining whether the treatment was less favourable.

We can see straightaway that in looking at comparative treatment the intent or motive of the alleged perpetrator can be determinative for claims of alleged sexual harassment involving a sexual motive but could add an additional hurdle in claims involving alleged unlawful acts of discrimination which are sexist rather than sexual in tenor.

Reed and Bull Information Systems Limited v Stedman [1999] IRLR 299

This case made the point that when examining whether or not sexual harassment has taken place an Employment Tribunal should not carve up each claim into a series of specific incidents and examine each incident's impact individually. The EAT quoted an American case heard in the US Federal court which stated that:

> *"the trier of fact must keep in mind that each successive episode has its predecessors, that the impact of the separate incidents may accumulate and that the work environment may exceed the sum of individual episodes."*

In short, an Employment Tribunal should look at the cumulative effect of the incidents rather than each incident individually.

Driskel v Peninsula Business Services Limited [2000] IRLR 151

Mrs Driskel was employed by Peninsula who somewhat ironically are a large, well-established provider of employment law advice and representation to employers.

The Employment Tribunal dismissed Mrs Driskel's claim of sexual harassment, even though the Employment Tribunal had found that a manager at Peninsula, a Mr Huss, had asked Mrs Driskel to wear a *"short skirt and see through blouse showing plenty of cleavage"* if she wanted to be successful at a job interview. Mr Huss had also made other comments of a sexual nature to Mrs Driskel.

The Employment Tribunal dismissed the comments as flippant and banter and accepted that Mrs Driskel had not raised any complaint at the time the comments were made or even taken the comments seriously.

The EAT disagreed with the Employment Tribunal's analysis and suggested that individual comments should not be viewed in isolation but the impact of the totality of successive incidents, however trivial, should be examined.

A Tribunal should not lose sight of the *"significance in this context of the sex of both the complainant and the alleged discriminator."*

What should be looked at by an Employment Tribunal is not whether the remark was *"flippant"* but whether it undermined the dignity of the recipient, a woman. The Employment Tribunal had also fallen into error by finding that Mr Huss 'made sexually vulgar comments to male employees. Sexually vulgar comments towards male employees would not have had the same impact as sexually vulgar comments to female employees.

Is a single incident enough?

The Tribunal and EAT held in ***Bracebridge Engineering Ltd v Darby*** *[1990] IRLR 3* that one incident of sexual harassment was enough to amount to sex discrimination.

Similarly in **Insitu Cleaning Co Ltd & Anor v Heads** [1994] UKEAT an Owner and Director said to a cleaner, who was twice his age, in a boardroom in front of others, "Hiya Big Tits." One incident was enough and that incident amounted to sex discrimination. The fact that Mrs Heads was upset, embarrassed and distressed by the comment amounted to a detriment. The fact that the perpetrator did not intend to upset, humiliate or embarrass only went to the gravity of the unlawful act not whether the act was unlawful.

Comments that are sexist in nature rather than sexual can amount to sexual harassment.

The role of the EU in defining harassment as a discrete form of discrimination

In 2000 the EC introduced the Equal Treatment Directive which member states were required to implement into their domestic law. The Directive required member states to introduce laws forbidding discrimination on grounds of sexual orientation, age, religion and belief. Furthermore, the Directive defined harassment as a form of discrimination.

The Directive had the following definition of harassment:

> *Harassment shall be deemed to be a form of discrimination within the meaning of paragraph 1, when unwanted conduct related to any of the grounds referred to in Article 1 takes place with the purpose or effect of violating the dignity of a person and of creating an intimidating, hostile, degrading, humiliating or offensive environment. In this*

context, the concept of harassment may be defined in accordance with the national laws and practice of the Member States.

Article one referred to the following grounds:

The purpose of this Directive is to lay down a general framework for combating discrimination on the grounds of religion or belief, disability, age or sexual orientation as regards employment and occupation, with a view to putting into effect in the Member States the principle of equal treatment.

Regulations were introduced in England Wales which prohibited discrimination on grounds of religion, belief, age and sexual orientation. These regulations almost incorporated lock stock and barrel the definition of harassment given in the Directive.

The Race Relations Act 1976, Sex Discrimination Act 1975 and the Disability Discrimination Act 1995 were amended accordingly to insert the new type of discrimination, harassment:

Harassment was defined as follows in the Race Relations Act 1976:

1) A person subjects another to harassment in any circumstances relevant for the purposes of any provision referred to in section 1 (1B) where, on grounds of race or ethnic or national origins, he engages in unwanted conduct which has the purpose or effect of –

(a) violating that other person's dignity, or

(b) creating an intimidating, hostile, degrading, humiliating or offensive environment for him.

(2) Conduct shall be regarded as having the effect specified in paragraph (a) or (b) of subsection (1) only if, having regard to all the circumstances, including in particular the perception of that other person, it should reasonably be considered as having that effect.

The same definitions were applied to both the Sex Discrimination Act and the Disability Discrimination Act.

However the eagle eyed amongst you will note that there was crucial difference between the language of the directive defining harassment and the language of the domestic legislation. The Directive used the following formulation when defining harassment:

> *related to any of the grounds*

Domestic legislation used the following, slightly different formulation:

> *on grounds of*

A difference in wording between the EU Directive and domestic legislation has proved to be fertile ground for creating uncertainty in the ambit of the law. Over the years it has also required some linguistic gymnastics in the Courts to reconcile these differences so that alignment with EU law is achieved.

So it proved with cases that came before the courts following the changes in definition.

In English v Thomas Sanderson Blinds Limited [2005] EWCA Civ 1421

Mr English was employed under a contract for services by Thomas Sanderson. Throughout his engagement with the business he was subject to sexual innuendo by his colleagues to the effect that he was homosexual. Such innuendo included being called a faggot. The homosexuality label was applied because his colleagues thought that Mr English was a stereotypical homosexual in that he was living in Brighton and because when he was educated he had attended a boarding school. Mr English's colleagues did not genuinely believe Mr Sanderson was homosexual and Mr English accepted that they did not believe he was homosexual. His colleagues were applying a negative stereotype to Mr English's personal circumstances.

Both the Employment Tribunal and the Employment Appeal Tribunal accepted and found that Mr English did not come within the ambit of the then Employment Equality (Sexual Orientation) Regulations 2003. Those regulations were said to implement the EC Equal Treatment Framework Directive. The EAT accepted that Mr English's treatment would have been unlawful under the Directive but was not unlawful under the domestic regulations. The domestic regulations required harassment to be on the *"grounds"* of sexual orientation rather than *"related to"* sexual orientation which was the Directive's wording.

The Court of Appeal in a majority decision found for Mr English. In determining the issue they saw that the critical words were *"on grounds of sexual orientation"* and LJ Collins held that the treatment afforded to Mr English was on grounds of sexual orientation. LJ Collins stated:

> *"If one were to ask the question whether the repeated and offensive use of the word "faggot" in the circumstances of this case was conduct on grounds of sexual orientation the answer should be in the affirmative irrespective of the actual sexual orientation of the claimant or the perception of his sexual orientation by his tormentors...it is plainly irrelevant whether the claimant is actually of a particular sexual orientation ...it is not for the claimant to show he is homosexual, any more than the claimant in a racial discrimination case must prove he is Asian or a Jew."*

Nixon v Ross Coates Solicitors and another UKEAT/0108/10

The Employment Tribunal dismissed a claim of harassment where the allegation was based on gossip spread by the firm's HR Manager about whether the Claimant conceived her baby at the firm's Christmas party and gossip about the identity of the father. The Claimant was in a relationship with a solicitor at the firm but at the Christmas party became very amorous with the firm's IT manager, a Mr Wright.

The EAT found that gossip spread by the HR manager about the paternity of the Claimant's child was sufficient to create a hostile and intimidating atmosphere, sufficient for the Claimant to request to work from a different office.

The gossip related to pregnancy and was therefore gender related and accordingly amounted to harassment. The EAT found that the Employment Tribunal had taken a very dim view of the Claimant's conduct at the Christmas party and that view had *"leaked"* into their judgment.

Furthermore in the case of **Moonsar v Fiveways Express Transport Limited** [2005] **IRLR 9** the EAT found that three male colleagues who downloaded pornographic images in an office shared with the Claimant amounted to unwanted conduct which created an environment where her dignity was violated, notwithstanding the fact that the Claimant did not complain at the time and the images were not shared with her directly. This case emphasises the environment that was created by sexist actions and that environment was sufficient to be degrading and humiliating, despite the fact that the environment that was created was not aimed specifically at the Claimant.

One of the leading cases under the new definition was **Richmond Pharmacology v Dhaliwal** where the Claimant brought a claim for racial harassment when her manager made a comment that *"We will probably bump into each other in the future unless you are married off in India."* The claim was upheld and the employer appealed. The EAT held:

1. *The old law was constructed rather uncomfortably and apart from general observations was unlikely to assist.*

2. *There are two alternative bases of liability – purpose and effect. Most cases will be about effect.*

3. *An employer will only be liable if the proscribed consequence or effect has happened* ***and*** *it was reasonable for it to have happened. Therefore the question to be answered was whether it was reasonable for the Claimant to have believed that her dignity was violated. Someone who unreasonably is prone to take offence will not have been harassed in law.*

In cases of alleged harassment an Employment Tribunal should ask and answer the following questions:

(i) What were the actual words spoken ("the conduct")?

(ii) Was the conduct complained of unwanted?

(iii) If so, was it on the grounds of ethnic origin?

(iv) If so, did the conduct have the purpose, alternatively the effect, of violating the Claimant's dignity, or creating an intimidating, hostile, degrading, humiliating or offensive environment for her?

(v) If it had that effect, should it reasonably be considered as having that effect, having regard to all the circumstances, including in particular the perception of the Claimant?

The Equality Act 2010 brought most of the main discrimination legislation under one roof.

The Equality Act 2010 also introduced the concept of "protected characteristics." The protected characteristics in relation to harassment are:

- Age
- Disability
- Gender reassignment

- Race.
- Sex.
- Sexual Orientation.

The Equality Act 2010 defined harassment in three ways:

i) Unwanted conduct which is related to a protected characteristic which has the purpose or effect of creating an intimidating, hostile, degrading, humiliating or offensive atmosphere or violates dignity.

ii) Unwanted conduct of a sexual nature which has the purpose or effect of creating an intimidating, hostile, degrading, humiliating or offensive atmosphere or violates dignity.

iii) Being treated less favourably because they have submitted to or rejected sexual harassment or harassment related to sex or gender reassignment.

You can see that the first definition of harassment now aligns precisely with the underlying Equal Treatment Directive, in that the word *"on grounds of"* have been replaced by *"related to"* thereby closing the gap between the EU definition and the initial transposition into UK law.

There have been a number of cases since the passage of the Equality Act 2010 which have illustrated and clarified the reach of the law.

In **Smith v Ideal Shopping Direct Limited UKEAT/0590** the EAT allowed an appeal against an Employment Tribunal dismissing a complaint of harassment on grounds of sexual orientation.

Whilst the Claimant had been referred to, inter alia as *"Val's bitch," "Big Gay Wayne," and "Will"* a character in a TV show who was a drama queen. The Claimant had also been told that it was easier for him to work weekends as he was gay and had no family.

The Employment Tribunal was satisfied that taken in the abstract these words and comments were homophobic, in the context of this particular workplace, a TV studio, they were not homophobic, in particular because the claimant had paraded his sexuality loudly and vocally.

The EAT was satisfied that the Employment Tribunal had misdirected themselves in law by focussing on the intent of the language rather than the effect. They further misdirected themselves in law by, in terms, saying that a person who parades their particular characteristic could expect responses or comments back referring to sexuality. The EAT accepted that proposition in principle but said that where the comments and responses were offensive then that tipped the balance and harassment on grounds of sexual harassment was made out.

The EAT overturned the decision.

In **Pemberton v Right Reverend Inwood** [2018] **IRLR 542** the Reverend Canon Pemberton was an ordained priest of the Church of England. In 2013 he married his same sex partner. As a result, the Acting Bishop of Southwell and Nottingham revoked Canon Pemberton's permission to officiate [PTO] and declined to grant Canon Pemberton an Extra Parochial Ministry Licence [EPML]. The basis for the revocation and refusal to grant was that Pastoral Rules and Guidance in the Church of England stated that it was not legally possible for two persons of the same sex to marry nor was it possible for someone in holy orders to enter into a same sex marriage. Furthermore, in order to be granted a PTO, a clergyman needed to be of good standing.

Section 53 of the Equality Act prohibits discrimination by a "qualifications body." However paragraph 2 of schedule 9 provided a defence for employment for the "purposes of organised religion."

The Court of Appeal found that the revocation of the PTO and the denial of the EPML did not amount to harassment. The basis for that was that the conduct fell within the exception at schedule 9 and therefore could not have had the proscribed effect of violating the Canon's dignity.

Furthermore, it was reasonable to conclude that the Canon's dignity was not violated as there had been long discussions between the Acting Bishop and the Canon about the Canon's intention to marry. The Canon and the Bishop held opposing views which were known prior to the marriage. It was therefore not reasonable for the Canon to have considered himself harassed when as a result of his same sex marriage his PTO was revoked and his EPML was denied. Those consequences were known to him prior to him taking the decision to marry.

Lord Justice Underhill sitting in the Court of Appeal revisited the decision in Dhaliwal. He recognised that the definition of harassment in the Race Relations Act was different to the definition under the Equality Act 2010.

In particular under the Equality Act the conduct must only be *related to* the protected characteristic rather than *on the grounds of* the protected characteristic.

LJ Underhill reformulated the test he set out in Dhaliwal as a twofold test.

Namely a subjective test as to whether the Claimant perceived that his or her dignity had been violated by the conduct in question or an adverse environment created. If the Claimant did not perceive the conduct had that effect, then no harassment could be found. If the Claimant did perceive the conduct did have that effect then the objective test was whether it was reasonable for the conduct to have had that effect.

Applying that test to the facts of Canon Pemberton's claim it was understandable that Canon Pemberton found the Church of England's rules on same sex marriage as upsetting, however it was not reasonable for him to find for Canon Pemberton to regard his dignity as being violated or an adverse environment created in circumstances where the Church of England was applying its sincerely-held beliefs in a way expressly permitted by schedule 9 of the Equality Act 2010. The Bishop had communicated the decision on revoking the PTO and withholding the EPML in a non-aggravating way. Therefore whilst it was accepted that Canon Pemberton believed that his treatment related to his sexual orientation and that treatment for Canon Pemberton created an offensive and adverse environment, it was not reasonable, applying an objective test for Canon Pemberton to believe his treatment amounted to harassment relating to his sexual orientation, his treatment related to the rules of the Church being applied. Those rules were permitted and lawful.

In the case of **Mr F Ahmed v The Cardinal Hume Academies** the Claimant had dyspraxia and was unable to write for more than a few minutes at a time. The Claimant was a trainee teacher on the Teach First scheme. The Headteacher found out that the Claimant had difficulty with his handwriting and the Head decided to suspend him from his duties to allow time for further investigation.

The Claimant claimed that he was interrogated about his disability in a hostile, negative and dismissive manner at his suspension meeting. However, the Employment Tribunal concluded that whilst the meeting was conducted in a way that was unwanted by the Claimant, it was not reasonable for the Claimant to believe that the questioning and manner of the questioning to constitute harassment.

The Head Teacher had a school to run and the Claimant was responsible for teaching 19 lessons of Business Studies each week. The Claimant was newly appointed and the Head Teacher's discovery regarding Mr Ahmed's handwriting was made at the start of term. The Employment Appeal Tribunal agreed with the Employment Tribunal's reasoning and found that the guidance set out in Pemberton had been followed.

In the case of **Shanks v Health Board [2023] EAT 148,** during the Coronavirus pandemic, the respondent required employees to wear facemasks per Scottish Government regulations, which stemmed from the Coronavirus Act 2020. A catering assistant, the claimant, refused to comply and was summarily dismissed for gross misconduct. The employment tribunal dismissed her claim for unfair dismissal, and she appealed, arguing that the regulations mandating facemask use were beyond the Scottish Government's authority, as they fell under the exception for "medical treatment" outlined in the Act. The Employment Appeal Tribunal (EAT) rejected her appeal, stating that while "prophylactic" measures aim to prevent disease, they do not constitute "medical treatment" as defined in the Act. The EAT concluded that the exception was intended to prevent compulsory medical treatments, not to exclude health and safety measures like facemask requirements aimed at reducing virus transmission.

In **Blanc de Provence Ltd v Ha [2023] EAT 160**, a female tailor was dismissed for redundancy by male managers, under circumstances she found intimidating. She objected to a meeting with them alone, but they insisted, locking the door behind her while informing her of her redundancy. Following the meeting, she filed a harassment claim under the Equality Act, alleging she was treated unequally due to her sex. The tribunal upheld her claim, noting that the treatment she received would likely have differed had she been a man.

In the case of **Greasley-Adams v Royal Mail Group Ltd [2023] EAT 86**, a part-time driver for Royal Mail with Asperger's Syndrome, faced deteriorating relations with two colleagues who filed harassment complaints against him, which were upheld. He submitted his own grievance alleging bullying and harassment, but it was rejected. After bringing an employment tribunal claim for harassment, his claims were dismissed. He appealed, arguing that his dignity could be violated even without awareness of the unwanted conduct and that the tribunal had too narrowly focused on the context of the investigation. The Employment Appeal Tribunal (EAT) dismissed his appeal, stating that the harassment definition required awareness of the conduct for it to affect dignity.

In **Driscoll v V&P Global**, an executive assistant at a legal recruitment consultancy, resigned and alleged that the chief executive created a hostile work environment through racist and sexist comments and aggressive behavior, leading to her claim of constructive dismissal under the harassment provisions of the Equality Act 2010. After the tribunal struck out her constructive dismissal claim, the claimant appealed, arguing that this interpretation was inconsistent with EU anti-discrimination directives. The Employment Appeal Tribunal (EAT) partially allowed the appeal, stating that constructive dismissal could amount to harassment if it involved unwanted conduct related to a protected characteristic. The EAT emphasised that the tribunal should assess whether the defendant's conduct constituted harassment and whether the claimant's resignation was a response to such conduct, allowing for a reevaluation of her claims.

Third-Party Harassment

The Equality Act 2010 did initially outlaw third-party harassment. However, the section was repealed in 2012. Prior to the Equality Act 2010, there were a number of cases on third party harassment which set out the circumstances in which an employer may be held liable for actions of a third party whom the employer does not employ. There is a duty to prevent third-party harassment.

The leading case is **Burton and Rhule v De Vere Hotels Limited**.

Two waitresses were employed on a casual basis to wait tables at a Round Table dinner held in a De Vere Hotel. The guest speaker at the dinner was Bernard Manning. The hotel was aware that Bernard Manning had a reputation as a "blue" comedian who was not shy in making remarks about race and sex as part of his routine. At the conclusion of the dinner the two waitresses were asked by the management of the hotel whether they wished to volunteer to clear tables. The waitresses, both Afro-Caribbean, volunteered. The management of the hotel knew that Bernard Manning was due to speak at the same time as the tables were being cleared. Whilst Mr Manning was speaking he referred to the waitresses as "nigger," "wog" and "sambo". Furthermore, the guests at the dinner subjected the waitresses to sexual harassment of a physical and verbal nature. The Employment Tribunal dismissed the complaints of harassment on the basis that those who harassed the waitresses were not employed by the hotel and the hotel could not be liable for their actions.

The Employment Appeal Tribunal disagreed. Judge Smith held that as the hotel were aware of the nature of Bernard Manning's act it was reasonably foreseeable that the waitresses would be subject to harassment of either a sexual or racial nature and putting the waitresses in a position where they were vulnerable to harassment in the workplace did subject them to a detriment on racial grounds.

So given that third party harassment is not specifically covered as a defined type of harassment in the Equality Act 2010, there is no reason, in principle, why an employee or worker, who is subject to third party harassment could not rely on Burton and the direct discrimination and detriment provisions, which are mirrored in the Equality Act 2010 to bring a claim of third party harassment.

In any event there is likely to be a new duty for employers to prevent sexual harassment by third parties, scheduled to be implemented in 2026.

CHAPTER THREE

HARASSMENT AND BULLYING UNDER THE EQUALITY ACT 2010

We can see from the preceding chapter that workplace harassment has assumed a more central role in the legislation, moving from an undefined, unlawful act of direct discrimination, a detriment, to a specifically defined type of discrimination, harassment.

A Claimant initially had to prove that they had been less favourably treated on a proscribed ground and that the less favourable treatment they were subjected to amounted to a detriment. The use of the word less involved a comparison with an actual or hypothetical person who did not share that characteristic. Defences sometimes revolved round employers alleging that the perpetrator has treated all employees in the same way, badly. This became known as "the bastard's defence." The alleged perpetrator did not discriminate he or she was a complete bastard to everyone, they did not discriminate.

The EU's Equal Treatment Directive of 2000 moved the law on and provided a defined meaning for harassment as well as making it a form of discrimination. The directive was transposed into domestic legislation, albeit initially imperfectly with the use of "on grounds of". The Equality Act 2010 brought the UK definition of harassment in line with the EU definition. The legal test for harassment was initially set out in Dhaliwal and then tweaked by the same judge in Canon Pemberton to reflect the fact that domestic legislation now mirrored the underlying directive.

In this chapter we will examine how the law works in practice. How it imposes liability on individuals and their employers for acts of harassment on proscribed grounds in the workplace.

Who is in scope and covered by the Equality Act 2010?

The scope of the Equality Act 2010 is set out at section 83. It covers those who are in employment. Employment covers those who work under a contract of employment, a contract of apprenticeship or a contract personally to do work. We will use the term employee to cover all those bases.

Cases on employee status and worker status are a live topic as we move into the era of the gig economy. However given that in practice there is no difference between being a personal contractor or an employee under the discrimination legislation then there have not been many cases under the discrimination legislation where the differences have to be teased out.

Furthermore section 108 of the Equality Act 2010 covers those who **were** in employment and are harassed afterwards. The wording is as follows:

> *A person (A) must not harass another (B) if –*
>
> (a) *The harassment arises out of and is closely connected to a relationship which used to exist between them, and*
>
> (b) *Conduct of a description constituting the harassment, would if it occurred during the relationship, contravene this Act.*

The Equality Act 2010 like its predecessor legislation covers those in a principal/agency relationship. Sections 109 and 110 of the Equality Act 2010 cover the liability of employers, principals and agents.

Cases pre-Equality Act 2010 are still good law as the wording of the respective sections on principal/agency and employment have remain unchanged from their predecessor legislation. Two of the key cases are:

In **Harrods v Remick,** Harrods, the department store, had a number of concessions in store. These concessions were particular brands who had their own counter within Harrods and employ their own employees. In this case the pen maker, Schaeffer, had a concession in Harrods and employed staff on the Schaeffer counter.

All concession staff who work in Harrods for any concession employer were however subject to "store approval" by Harrods. Harrods either withdrew their approval or did not grant their approval to the Claimants in this case. In one case approval was not granted to an Asian concession employee because she wore a nose stud as part of her religion.

If Harrods did not approve any employee employed by the concession then the concession had to remove that employee from the Harrods store.

The Claimants brought claims for race discrimination against Harrods. The Employment Tribunal held that the Claimants were subject to race discrimination but also held that Harrods was not liable as the Claimants did not work for them and were not in their employment.

The EAT and the Court of Appeal disagreed and held that the Claimants whilst employed by the particular concessions worked for Harrods and came within the ambit of the Principal/Agent section of the Race Relations Act 1976.

In **Bates Von Winklehoff v Clyde and Co LLP [2014] UKSC 32** a member of a law firm's LLP was found to be a worker and protected by the whistleblowing legislation. The Supreme Court teased out the distinction between the differing protections for different types of contractors under the Employment Rights Act 1996, where the whistleblowing framework is found, and the Equality Act 2010 where the discrimination legislation is found.

> *As already seen, employment law distinguishes between three types of people: those employed under a contract of employment; those self-employed people who are in business on their own account and undertake work for their clients or customers; and an intermediate class of workers who are self-employed but do not fall within the second class. Discrimination law, on the other hand, while it includes a contract*

> *'personally to do work' within its definition of employment (see, now, Equality Act 2010, s.83(2)) does not include an express exception for those in business on their account who work for their clients or customers. But a similar qualification has been introduced by a different route.*

The writer of this book acted for an underwear model, Sonja Walker, who worked through a model agency – Premier Models. BHS, a department store, booked the client for a shoot on location in Norfolk. Whilst on the shoot the Claimant was sexually harassed by a BHS employee, Becki Hough.

The claim of harassment was brought against BHS and the alleged harasser, Becki Hough. Both the Employment Tribunal and the Employment Appeal Tribunal found that whilst on the shoot the Claimant was protected from discrimination as she was in the employment of BHS whilst the shoot was ongoing.

In what circumstances is a person in scope protected?

In order to be protected from an unlawful act of harassment on proscribed grounds in the workplace, the harassment has to have happened in the course of the harasser's employment.

In the course of employment has been broadly and purposively interpreted. It means whilst the harassed was applying for employment, in employment, or following his or her employment subject to the closely connected to test at section 108.

Section 108 of the Equality Act 2010 deals with relationships that have ended. If an employment relationship has ended and there is an act of harassment following the relationship ending, then the former employee will have a right to bring a claim if the harassment "*arises out of*" or is "*closely connected to a relationship that exists between them.*"

Section 109 of the Equality Act 2010 imposes liability on employers as follows:

> *Anything done by a person (A) in the course of A's employment must be treated as also done by the employer.*

As "*the course of employment*" wording has been a constant throughout the history of the discrimination legislation, cases that pre-date the Equality Act 2010 on this point are still good law.

The courts had had a number of cases to decide what in the course of employment means. Overall the cases have illustrated that in practice the scope of in the "course of employment" is wide ranging and Employment Tribunals will be slow to hold that an act is outside the course of employment if there is a causal nexus or connection between the act of harassment and the employment.

One of the leading cases is **Tower Boot Company Limited v Jones [1997] IRLR 168** in that case Mr Jones, aged just 16, worked for Tower Boot Company, a business that made shoes and that had not previously employed anyone other than white people. Whilst working there as a machine operative, Mr Jones, of mixed race but with an Afro-Caribbean parent, was subject to a campaign of bullying and racial harassment which included branding him with an iron, whipping him and subjecting him to offensive racial insults including calling him a "*baboon*". He left after a month.

The employers in the Employment Tribunal argued that the harassment was unauthorised and therefore they were not liable as unauthorised acts could not amount to being done in the course of employment. The Tribunal rejected that argument and awarded Mr Jones £5,000.00 compensation for the racial harassment.

The employers appealed. The EAT held that:

> *"The EAT majority said the phrase "in the course of employment" had "a well-established meaning in law". The "nub of the test" as set out in Salmond on Torts is "whether the unauthorised wrongful act of the servant is so connected with that which he was employed to do as to be a mode of doing it". In this case, according to the EAT majority, the acts complained of, including the deliberate branding with a hot screwdriver and whipping, could not be described, by any stretch of the imagination, as an improper mode of performing authorised tasks."*

The employee appealed and the Court of Appeal found in favour of his appeal.

The Court of Appeal held that the words in the course of employment should be given their ordinary and every day meaning rather than be interpreted by way of the meaning ascribed to those words in Tort.

Furthermore as the mischief of racial and sexual harassment was pernicious it was necessary to take a purposive approach to ensure that employees and workers had protection in the workplace.

The employers could always rely on the reasonably practicable steps defence if they had taken proactive steps to prevent employees from racially harassing one another. Therefore the employees who racially harassed Mr Jones were acting in the course of their employment and the employers were therefore liable for those employees' harassment of Mr Jones.

In the case of **The Chief Constable of Lincolnshire Police and others v Stubbs [1999] ICR 547** a Police Constable was subject to sexual harassment whilst off duty with colleagues in a public house. The male colleague, also a police officer, subjected Ms Stubbs to sexual harassment. One of the key points decided in the appeal by the Court of Appeal was whether a social occasion whilst off duty could amount to in the course of employment.

The Employment Appeal Tribunal held that it could, and the employer was therefore liable for the acts of harassment. In deciding that issue the EAT held:

> "*We concur with the findings of the industrial tribunal, that the two incidents referred to, although "social events" away from the police station, were extensions of the work place. Both incidents were social gatherings involving officers either immediately after work or for an organised leaving party. They come within the definition of course of employment, as recently interpreted by the Court of Appeal in Jones v. Tower Boot Co. Ltd. [1997] I.C.R. 254 and Waters v. Commissioner of Police of the Metropolis [1997] I.C.R. 1073. It would have been different as it seems to us had the discriminatory acts occurred during a chance meeting between Detective Sergeant Walker and the applicant at a supermarket, for example, but, when there is a social gathering of work colleagues such as there was in this case, it is entirely appropriate for the tribunal to consider whether or not the circumstances show that what was occurring was an extension of their employment. It seems to us that each case will depend upon its own facts. The borderline may be difficult to find. It is a question of the good exercise of judgment by an industrial jury. Whether a person is or is not on duty, and whether or not the conduct occurred on the employer's premises, are but two of the factors which will need to be considered. On the facts of this case, the industrial tribunal well understood that the applicant was not and could not be thought to have been socialising with Detective Sergeant Walker on either of those two occasions. Indeed, it would appear from their decision, that this was the last thing that she would have been wishing to do. It seems to us that the way it was put in Jones v. Tower Boot Co. Ltd. [1997] I.C.R. 254, 265, succinctly sets out the task of the industrial tribunal*"

As we can see the Courts have taken a wide and purposive approach to whether an act of alleged harassment took place in the course of employment.

I represented in a case where the employer sought to argue that text messages sent by a manager to a female employee who was in a subordinate position did not happen in the course of employment as they were sent outside of work hours and were sent to a private mobile number. The texts sent were found to be in the course of employment, notwithstanding the fact that the texts were sent on a private phone and over the weekend.

Can an individual perpetrator be individually liable for an unlawful act of harassment?

Yes, the Equality Act 2010 is predicated on the idea that individuals are individually liable for their actions. Individuals discriminate. Employers are liable for any employee or worker who discriminates against another whilst the discriminator is in the employer's employment.

Section 109 states that anything done by a person in their course of their employment is treated as done by their employer and section 109 (3) states that

> *"It does not matter whether that thing is done with the employer's knowledge or approval."*

Does an Employer have a defence in the Equality Act 2010?

An employer does have a statutory defence under section 109 (4) of the Equality Act 2010 if the employer has taken all reasonably practicable steps to prevent A from doing the unlawful act. We will examine the defences in further detail in the last chapter.

Furthermore if the reasonably practicable steps defence is made out the individual can be individually liable for their own discrimination.

An example of an individual being made liable for their individual act of harassment is the case of racial harassment brought against a Mr Hossack by a Mr Leader in the Leeds Employment Tribunal. Mr Hossack's employer Leeds City Council was dismissed from proceedings when the Claimant accepted that Leeds City Council had taken all reasonably practicable steps to prevent Mr Hossack from making racist comments. Leeds City Council's defence under section 109 (4) had been made out.

Mr Hossack was found to have made the racist comments to Mr Leader and the Employment Tribunal ordered Mr Hossack to pay Mr Leader the sum of £2,500.00 as compensation for injury to feelings.

If the statutory defence is not made out by the employer and the claim is brought against both the harasser and their employer then liability is imposed on a joint and several basis. We will look at that in more detail when we look at remedies.

In practical terms if a person believes they have been discriminated against or harassed they have the choice of bringing a claim against:

1. The alleged discriminator's or harasser's employer or;

2. The alleged discriminator or harasser as an individual and the alleged discriminator's or harasser's employer.

If option 2 is chosen and a claim is brought against both the alleged harasser and their employer, the Claimant will have to start early conciliation against both with ACAS and obtain an early conciliation certificate against both the individual and their employer.

Once early conciliation certificates have been issued a Claimant usually has 30 days to issue a claim in Employment Tribunal.

In what timeframe does a claim have to be brought?

Section 123(1) of the Equality Act 2010 imposes a time limit of 3 months to bring a claim "*starting with the date of the act to which the complaint relates.*"

Usually cases of harassment are cases involving a course of conduct and the 3-month time limit runs from the last alleged incident of harassment.

An Employment Tribunal does have jurisdiction to hear a claim brought outside the 3-month time limit if it is just and equitable to hear the claim late. The just and equitable discretion involves the Employment Tribunal weighing a number of factors before arriving at a conclusion.

The factors that are weighed are:

1. Reason for the delay.
2. Length of the delay.
3. The presence or absence of any prejudice to the respondent if the claim is allowed to proceed (other than the prejudice involved in having to defend proceedings).
4. The presence or absence of any other remedy for the claimant if the claim is not allowed to proceed.
5. The conduct of the respondent subsequent to the act of which complaint is made, up to the date of the application.
6. The conduct of the claimant over the same period;
7. The length of time by which the application is out of time.
8. The medical condition of the Claimant, taking into account, in particular, any reason why this should have prevented or inhibited the making of a claim;

9. The extent to which professional advice on making a claim was sought and, if it was sought, the content of any advice given.

How does an internal procedure impact on time?

In **Aniagwu (appellant) v. (1) London Borough of Hackney and (2) Owens** the Employment Tribunal had to consider the effect of an internal procedure on time. The Claimant was denied a top up car loan by his manager. He believed that refusal was made on racial grounds. He lodged a grievance in March. That grievance was dismissed. He then appealed against the grievance outcome. The appeal was not dealt with in a timely manner and was dismissed in June. Thereafter he lodged an Employment Tribunal claim for race discrimination. The Employment Tribunal held that time ran from the date of the rejection of the original grievance, March, and found the claim to be out of time and it was not just and equitable to hear the claim.

Mr Aniagwu appealed. The EAT found that the Employment Tribunal's judgment contained an error of law.

The EAT held that time ran from the rejection of the internal appeal and that although the claim was still presented one day out of time from that date it was nevertheless just and equitable to hear the claim.

The EAT held:

> *In finding that it was not just and equitable to extend the time limit for presenting the applicant's race discrimination complaint, the employment tribunal erred in failing to consider the reason why the complaint was not presented earlier.*
>
> *Unless there is some particular feature about the case or some particular prejudice which the employers can show, every tribunal would inevitably conclude that it is a responsible and proper attitude for someone to seek*

to redress a grievance through the employer's internal grievance procedure before embarking on legal proceedings.

In the present case, there was nothing to indicate that the employers would have been prejudiced in any way by an extension of time. The appeal would be allowed and a declaration made that it was just and equitable that the application should be determined.

If a claim is brought within time then an Employment Tribunal will have jurisdiction to hear the claim.

Constitution of the Employment Tribunal

If a claim of harassment in the workplace is made, the Claimant can bring their claim in the Employment Tribunal on form ET1. Prior to bringing the claim the Claimant will have to have an ACAS Early Conciliation certificate for each party against whom the claim is brought.

The employer will lodge their defence on form ET3. The claim will go through the normal timetabling in terms of disclosure of documents, production of an evidence bundle and exchange of witness statements. Once all the pre-hearing orders have been complied with the claim goes to hearing.

Any claim for discrimination has to be heard by a full Employment Tribunal panel – that means an Employment Judge who is there to guide on the law as well as two lay members drawn from either side of the industrial fence – one lay member will have a Trade Union background, the other a Human Resources background. It is usually not difficult to identify which lay member comes from which background.

In claims of sex discrimination or sexual harassment it is usual for the panel to have at least one woman on it. In claims of race discrimination or racial harassment it is normal to have one member of the panel drawn from an ethnic minority.

The Employment Tribunal's role is to act as an Industrial Jury. To find what the facts are and then to apply the law to those facts.

Like any system of determining a legal outcome by a jury, baked into the system is a recognition that two different juries could come to the opposite conclusions on the same evidence. People do interpret events in different ways. When weighing evidence and credibility of evidence different people react differently to the same evidence. That's inevitable. That's why lawyers talk of litigation risk as the risk is always there that evidence either may not come out the way you expect or may be received in a way that is unexpected.

What is the burden of proof?

If a claim is present to the Employment Tribunal, the Employment Tribunal's role is to decide the claim and apply a burden of proof.

Whilst the burden of proof is on the Claimant, following King v Great Britain China Centre Employment Tribunals recognise that discriminators rarely admit discrimination, even to themselves.

The Claimant has to bring a prima facie case after which the burden of proof switches and the Employer has to satisfy the Tribunal that their explanation for the treatment is not on a proscribed ground.

In harassment claims, the fact finding is usually between two opposing accounts. The Claimant alleging that they were harassed. The Respondent alleging either that the alleged acts of harassment did not take place or that the alleged acts of harassment did not have the alleged harassing effect on the Claimant, that the surrounding context suggests that the conduct was not intimidatory, unwanted or hostile. Dirt is thrown. The Employment Tribunal's role is to determine who that dirt sticks to.

The Employment Tribunal has to make findings on the evidence before it. The Employment Tribunal's role is to make findings of fact, apply the law to those findings of fact and then reach a judgment based on the findings and the application of the law. The Employment Tribunal cannot fence sit. Fence sitting is an abdication of responsibility. A case we did at PJH Law illustrates the point.

A female employee at a petrol station along the A1 alleged that she was sexually harassed by the owner. The Employer denied harassment had taken place. The claim went to Bury St Edmunds Employment Tribunal before Employment Judge Cole, a meticulously fair and courteous Judge, in our firm's experience. Employment Judge Cole and his two members sitting with him decided that they could not resolve the conflict of evidence. The Tribunal did not know whom to believe. As the evidence in the Employment Tribunal's view did not come up to the required proof, the claim was dismissed. Our client appealed. The EAT upheld the appeal and stated that it is the Employment Tribunal's job to make findings on the evidence and in failing to make a decision and failing to make findings the Employment Tribunal had abdicated their responsibility.

What types of remedy are available to a successful Claimant?

1. A Declaration

If an Employment Tribunal finds that an unlawful act of harassment has taken place, the Employment Tribunal can make a declaration to that effect. For many, if not all Claimants, this declaration is one of the most important remedies. The Claimant has been believed and has had their claim upheld.

An Employment Tribunal in making their judgement have preferred the Claimant's evidence to the perpetrator's evidence and any evidence from their employer's. That finding is normally a substantial remedy for the

Claimant on its own. Quite often a Claimant will have lodged a grievance with their employer and not been believed.

Furthermore a finding of harassment made by an Employment Tribunal will normally have been made after a Claimant's evidence has been thoroughly tested both under cross examination and by any questions the Employment Tribunal may have.

In our experience as practitioners at the sharp end an Employment Tribunal making a finding of harassment can substantially impact in a positive way on the well-being of a Claimant.

Many victims of harassment lose self-confidence – that loss of self-confidence can be aggravated further if an employer rejects a grievance lodged by the employee. With that loss of self-confidence well-being and health are also affected as collateral damage.

Bringing a claim alleging harassment takes inordinate courage. That courage is found when the victim of harassment is already at a very low point.

In the Sonja Walker case the then Chairman of BHS, Philip Green, rang me up and told me my client "had a bolt loose." That sort of clumsy attempt to undermine and denigrate a person bringing a claim of harassment is not unusual. Usually it has the opposite effect of the one intended. Both the victim of harassment and their lawyer's resolve hardens in the face of an attempt to bully and to intimidate.

A declaration of harassment amounts to a huge weight being lifted from the Claimant's shoulders – in our experience that weight being lifted usually results in a spring in a successful Claimant's step and a return of confidence and well-being.

The most important remedy is therefore a declaration that the Claimant has been harassed.

It is worth noting that all Employment Tribunal's decisions are now online for the public to view.

A finding of harassment is damaging for an organisation's reputation and it is even more damaging to the reputation of the perpetrator who will have their acts of harassment found as such and published online in a document that can be found with a google search.

Many organisations who tender for public sector work have to complete a tender document that asks about whether the organisation has had any discrimination claims. There is therefore a strong incentive for organisations not to allow harassment in the workplace and not to have been found by an Employment Tribunal to have allowed harassment at work.

2. Compensation

An employment tribunal can award a remedy that is just and equitable and takes account of the losses flowing from the discrimination. There are a number of elements to compensation.

2.1 Compensation Awards

Up until 1993 discrimination awards including awards for acts of harassment were capped at the level of unfair dismissal awards which was then £12,000.00. A case that was appealed to the European Court of Justice changed all that. Following the case of ***Marshall v Southampton and South-West Hampshire Area Health Authority (No 2)*** **[1993] IRLR 445, [1993] ICR 893** *the European Court of Justice found that the limits on compensation found in the Sex Discrimination Act 1976 were unlawful and did not comply with the underlying Directive. Accordingly the Sex Discrimination Act and Race Relations Act were amended to bring them into line with EU law, notwithstanding the fact that EU law did not apply then* *to Race Relations. As a result compensation caps were taken off. Compensation for acts of discrimination or harassment are unlimited*

Compensation can be awarded for losses flowing from the discriminatory act of harassment. If the harassment has led to the loss of the job because the employee or worker has left as a result then the compensation can cover loss of income until another job is found.

It would be unusual for an act of harassment to itself be an express dismissal by the employer but it is possible. We have dealt with cases where a female employee has been subjected to unwanted sexual advances only to be subsequently dismissed for an apparently unrelated but sham reason.

It is far more likely that the harassment will lead to a constructive dismissal either because the employee resigns in response to the harassment or lodges a grievance and resigns in response to an unsatisfactory outcome. In either event an act of harassment will amount to a repudiatory breach of contract entitling an employee to resign and claim constructive dismissal.

The writer represented in an Employment Tribunal case that established a constructive dismissal is covered by the discrimination legislation that predated the Equality Act 2010 in **Derby Specialist Fabrications Limited v Burton [2001] ICR 833** where it held that racial harassment that went unchecked by the employer could give grounds for a constructive dismissal and a dismissal on those grounds would be on racial grounds and therefore discriminatory:

> *We agree with that approach. An Employment Tribunal in such cases should have regard to the totality of a number of successive incidents, because there may well be a cumulative effect. If looking at them overall as a breach of contract they can be seen to be or inferred to be based on racial grounds, so that the complainant would have been treated differently but for his race, then the repudiation by the employer of the contract of employment is to be treated as racially discriminatory. Such*

*racial grounds must, of course, amount to a substantial cause of the employer's actions or his inactions. They must be an important reason for them, but they need not be the sole reason; **Owen & Briggs v James [1982] IRLR 502.***

The tribunal in this present case seems to have arrived at such an overall conclusion about the totality of the matters which it regarded as amounting to constructive dismissal. It was not required to make express findings of racial grounds for each of the individual acts. We cannot see that it went wrong in law in the approach which it adopted.

Of course the employee or worker has to mitigate their loss by looking for work that produces an income either on an employed or self-employed basis.

2.2 Injury to Feelings

An act of harassment causes an employee to be upset, humiliated, offended or can cause illness. An injury to feelings award attempts to compensate for the upset caused.

Injury to feelings awards are banded into one of three bands called the Vento bands.

Band one, the lowest band, is for harassment (or discrimination) which has upset and or distressed the Claimant but has had no adverse health effects.

Band two, the middle band, is for harassment which has upset and or distressed the Claimant and has adversely affected the Claimant in a demonstrable way, usually backed up by medical evidence proving that the acts of harassment has caused the Claimant ill health.

Band three, the upper band, is the highest band. A Claimant will be awarded an injury to feelings award in the upper band if the act of harassment has caused psychiatric injury. Again the Claimant will have to prove the effect on health by putting medical evidence before the Employment Tribunal. The medical evidence will have to show that the harassment caused the ill health. There has to be a causal link.

The current bandings for Vento injury to feeling awards for acts of discrimination occurring after March 2019 are between £900.00 and £44,000.00. The bandings are up-rated regularly:

1) Band one between £900.00 and £8,800.00.

2) Band two, the middle band, between £8,800.00 and £26,300.00.

3) Band three, the upper band, between £26,300.00 and £44,000.00.

2.3 Personal Injury

An Employment Tribunal can make an award for personal injury if the act of harassment caused personal injury. The case of **Sheriff v Klyne Tugs (Lowestoft) 1999 ICR 1170** established that an Employment Tribunal has the same right to award damages for personal injury for the tort of harassment as a County Court.

The wording of the section on remedy in the Equality Act 2010 at section 124 (6) allows an Employment Tribunal to award compensation that could be awarded by the County Court.

Therefore if psychiatric harm is caused by an act of harassment then an award for injury to feelings will be made in the upper band.

Additionally if the psychiatric harm has caused other losses, such as an inability to work and earn an income, then an Employment Tribunal can make an award of compensation for all losses flowing from the act of harassment. The losses do not have to reasonably foreseeable but just caused by or flowing from the harassment.

In the case of **HM Prison Service v Salmon [2001] IRLR 425** an Employment Tribunal found the Claimant to have been subjected to sexual harassment in the workplace. The offending conduct was writing sexually derogatory comments about the Claimant in the Canterbury Crown Court dock book. Mrs Salmon suffered a moderate to severe depressive episode and eventually left the prison service under a medical retirement.

The Employment Tribunal awarded £45,000.00 for loss of earnings, £20,000.00 for injury to feelings and also awarded £11,250.00 compensation for personal injury in respect of the psychiatric damage caused to Mrs Salmon.

The figure for personal injury was arrived at by assessing "full" compensation for her injury at £15,000, on the basis that her illness fell within the category of "moderately severe" psychiatric damage as defined in the 1998 edition of the Judicial Studies Board Guidelines for personal injury damages, for which a bracket of £9,500 to £27,500 is given. The tribunal then reduced the £15,000 by 25% on the basis that her depressive illness was only caused to the extent of 75% by the acts of discrimination which had been proved. The prison service appealed the level of award. The EAT dismissed the appeal and had this to say about recovery of damages for personal injury:

> *The overlap between the injury to feelings for which the applicant would be compensated and the injury covered by the award of general damages for psychiatric injury was not such as to give rise to a substantial degree of double recovery.*
>
> *In principle, injury to feelings and psychiatric injury are distinct. In practice, however, the two types of injury are not always easily separable, giving rise to a risk of double recovery. In a given case, it may be impossible to say with any certainty or precision when the distress and humiliation that may be inflicted on the victim of discrimination becomes a recognised psychiatric illness such as depression. Injury to feelings can cover a very wide range. At the lower*

end are comparatively minor instances of upset or distress, typically caused by one-off acts or episodes of discrimination. At the upper end, the victim is likely to be suffering from serious and prolonged feelings of humiliation, low self-esteem and depression; and in these cases it may be fairly arbitrary whether the symptoms are put before the tribunal as a psychiatric illness, supported by a formal diagnosis and/or expert evidence.

2.4 Aggravated Damages

An Employment Tribunal can make an award of aggravated damages in certain circumstances. The test for whether an award of aggravated damages has been met is set out in the HM Prison Service v Salmon case referred to above. Quoting from the EAT judgment:

"It is convenient to start with the question of aggravated damages. It has been clear since the decision of the Court of Appeal in Alexander v Home Office [1988] IRLR 190 that it is open to a tribunal in a discrimination case to include in its 'compensatory' award

... an element of aggravated damages where, for example, the defendants may have behaved in a high-handed, malicious, insulting or oppressive manner in committing the act of discrimination'.

see per May LJ at p.193. However, it is also clear that aggravated damages are awarded only on the basis, and to the extent, that the aggravating features have increased the impact of the discriminatory act or conduct on the applicant and thus the injury to his or her feelings: in other words, they form part of the compensatory award and do not constitute a separate, punitive, award."

In the case of Geraghty v Forose [2023] NICA, the Tribunal award of £6,000 was found to be unimpeachable where the employer had sexually harassed a 15-year-old employee, 40 years younger than him. Mr Geraghty had been prosecuted but had defended all proceedings in an aggravating manner, degrading the Claimant as a "scam artist,"

2.5 Stigma Damages

In Chagger v Abbey National Plc and another [2009] EWCA Civ 1202 the Court of Appeal had to look at whether stigma damages were recoverable as a separate head of loss in a discrimination claim.

The facts were that Mr Chagger worked in financial services for Abbey National. His selection for redundancy was found to be discriminatory. Mr Chagger was marked down on one criteria because of his race.

Mr Chagger engaged with over 20 employment agencies, applied for many jobs but could not find any employment within his sector, financial services. Mr Chagger stated in evidence that his claim against Abbey National had stigmatised him in the jobs market.

The Employment Tribunal awarded Mr Chagger over two million pounds in compensation on the basis that but for the discrimination he would have remained in employment with Abbey National. The Tribunal accepted Mr Chagger's schedule of loss which amounted to over four million to an extent but reduced the compensation awarded based on chances that Mr Chagger would not have earnt the sum claimed.

The case ended up in the Court of Appeal. Abbey National argued that if Mr Chagger was stigmatised in the market because he had brought a claim for race discrimination against Abbey National then Mr Chagger had a legal right to bring a claim for victimisation against those prospective employers who had not employed him because of bringing a claim against Abbey.

Mr Chagger argued that the stigma in the employment market flowed from the act of discrimination and that Abbey should be liable for the stigma and the unemployability arising from the stigma.

Pausing there, many of us will have heard anecdotally that if an employee brings a legal claim against an employer in the City of London, that employee runs the risk of never working in the City again. The City like many sectors is a networked environment where many senior people in separate organisations know one another and news travels.

The Court of Appeal accepted that in principle stigma loss was recoverable, notwithstanding the fact that an employee may also have a separate legal claim against a prospective employer for victimisation. The Court of Appeal's rationale was as follows:

> *An important feature, in our view, is that it can be very difficult for an employee to make good his suspicions that he is subject to unlawful victimisation discrimination, and he ought not to be criticised for being reluctant or unwilling to devote the time, money and stress necessary to advance that claim. Furthermore, we doubt whether Parliament in passing the victimisation provisions intended thereby to weaken the extent of the protection which the discriminated victim would have against his own employer.*
>
> *It is also material to note that it is only in the context of discrimination laws that the concept of victimisation discrimination has been developed. Each of the discrimination statutes provides for a free standing wrong of victimisation, but it is not always unlawful for third party employers to refuse to recruit someone who has sued his own employer. For example, an employee who has taken proceedings for unfair dismissal could be stigmatised in that way quite lawfully. It would be unsatisfactory and somewhat artificial if tribunals were obliged to discount stigma loss in the context of discrimination law but not in other contexts.*
>
> *In our judgment the stigma loss is in principle recoverable. It is one of the difficulties facing an employee on the labour market.*

The next question for the Court of Appeal was how should stigma damages be assessed? The Court of Appeal said that ordinarily stigma damages should not be awarded as a separate head of loss. An Employment Tribunal should have in mind that some Claimants may experience stigma in the marketplace for bringing a claim and that stigma should be borne in mind when assessing the length of time loss should be awarded for. The only exception to the rule that stigma should not be a separate head of loss is where the Employer can show that the employee would have been dismissed at some point in the future fairly and without discrimination. In that exceptional case the Employee can have a separate head of future loss which claims stigma in the market for bringing a claim that will affect future employability and cause loss, notwithstanding the point that the Employer could have fairly and non-discriminatorily dismissed before the point the loss caused by the stigma arises.

2.6 Exemplary Damages

Discrimination and Harassment under the Equality Act 2010 are a tort, a wrongdoing. The employee responsible for the wrongdoing can be liable for their actions and their employer can be vicariously liable for their employee's wrongdoing.

Compensation for tort is based on losses flowing from the wrongdoing. Exemplary damages are damages to punish the wrongdoer and in terms make an example of him and her. Exemplary damages are not usually awarded in cases of Tort or Discrimination. However exemplary damages are payable in Tort in two exceptional circumstances identified by Lord Denning in the case of Rookes v Barnard. Firstly where the wrongdoer is in public office and has acted in a way that is misfeasance in public office. Secondly exemplary damages are payable where the wrongdoer has sought to make a profit from his wrongdoing and such a profit could exceed the losses incurred by his victim.

In the case of **Kuddus v Chief Constable of Leicestershire Constabulary [2001] UKHL 29** the House of Lords reconsidered the issue of exemplary damages in a claim brought against the Police. The House of Lords held that in principle exemplary damages are payable for Torts that did not exist when Rookes v Barnard was decided, for example discrimination law and the laws around Data Protection. It was the features of the tort rather than the tort itself which was determinative as to whether exemplary damages could be payable. However exemplary damages could only be payable either if the wrongdoer was in public office and committing an act of misfeasance or if the wrongdoer sought to profit from their wrongdoing.

In principle therefore in a Monica Lewinsky type situation where a public office holder was abusing their position to harass subordinates an award of exemplary damages could be payable for harassment. The second type of situation is where the harasser seeks to profit personally from their harassment. Profit personally implies an element of financial profit rather than personal profit by way of sexual gratification.

The exemplary damages will be payable by the wrong doer and the issue of whether the employer of the wrong doer would be liable for payment is very much a live issue and not one that was determined by the House of Lords.

In theory then exemplary damages could be payable for acts of harassment. Such awards will be exceptional though.

2.7 Statutory Adjustments

Adjustments to awards of up to 25% can be made by Employment Tribunals in a limited set of circumstances. Similarly awards can be decreased by up to 25% in a limited set of circumstances.

During the Blair government in the early part of this twenty first century statutory procedures were introduced. Employers had to comply with these procedures when dealing with grievances, similarly employees had to use the procedure if they had a grievance. Employers had to dismiss employees in a way that was compliant with the statutory dismissal procedure.

Whilst the intention of the introduction of such statutory procedures was good, to promote best practice and avoid legal disputes, the procedures caused more problems than they solved. There were many reported cases on whether or not the statutory procedure had been followed. The statutory procedures were eventually scrapped. Eventually to incentivise best practice and punish worst practice the Employment Act 2008 was amended to allow Employment Tribunals to increase or decrease awards according to whether the relevant ACAS Code of Practice had been followed. The relevant sections are at section 207A of the TULRCA:

> *This section applies to proceedings before an employment tribunal relating to a claim by an employee under any of the jurisdictions listed in Schedule A2.*
>
> *(2) If, in the case of proceedings to which this section applies, it appears to the employment tribunal that—*
>
> *(a) the claim to which the proceedings relate concerns a matter to which a relevant Code of Practice applies,*
>
> *(b) the employer has failed to comply with that Code in relation to that matter, and*
>
> *(c) that failure was unreasonable,*
>
> *the employment tribunal may, if it considers it just and equitable in all the circumstances to do so, increase any award it makes to the employee by no more than 25%.*
>
> *(3) If, in the case of proceedings to which this section applies, it appears to the employment tribunal that—*
>
> *(a) the claim to which the proceedings relate concerns a matter to which a relevant Code of Practice applies,*
>
> *(b) the employee has failed to comply with that Code in relation to that matter, and*

(c) that failure was unreasonable,

the employment tribunal may, if it considers it just and equitable in all the circumstances to do so, reduce any award it makes to the employee by no more than 25%.

The key issue here therefore is the adjustment provisions may apply if the employee has not brought a grievance alleging harassment. If the employee has not brought a grievance alleging harassment then the award for any harassment could be reduced by up to 25% if the failure to bring a grievance was unreasonable. There may be all sorts of reasons why failing to bring a grievance for alleged acts of harassment will not be unreasonable, particularly in organisations that are small to medium sized.

Conversely if an employee brings a grievance alleging harassment and the employer fails to deal with the grievance in accordance with the ACAS Code of Practice then the employer may be liable for an uplift of up to 25% for failing to deal with the grievance properly.

Further a failure to prevent harassment of a sexual nature will result in an uplift of up to 25%.

2.8 Interest

One of the other implications of the Marshall case referred to above was that the law was amended to allow for interest on discrimination awards. The upshot was that as from 1996 Employment Tribunals could award interest on an injury to feelings award for discrimination from the date that the incident occurred to the date of hearing. An Employment Tribunal could also award interest for compensation other than injury to feeling from the mid-point in time from when the discrimination occurred to when the award is made and the interest calculated. Interest can be ordered to payable for half the time between the act of harassment and the calculation date.

In **Derby Specialist Fabrications Limited v Burton** [2001] **IRLR 69** a case in which the writer acted as Solicitor in the Employment Tribunal the EAT held:

> *The employment tribunal did not err in awarding interest on its award of £5,000 compensation for injury to feelings so as to cover the whole of the period during which injury to feelings had taken place, in accordance with reg. 6(1)(a) of the Employment Tribunals (Interest on Awards etc) Regulations. The tribunal did not arrive at a perverse conclusion in deciding not to exercise its powers under reg. 6(3) to award interest from the midpoint of the date the discrimination began and the date of the award on grounds that "serious injustice" would be caused if interest was to be awarded from the date of the act of discrimination.*
>
> *The mere fact that an award for injury to feelings reflects injury occurring over a period of time cannot of itself justify a departure from the normal rule in reg. 6(1)(a). It is clear that Parliament intended that, unlike interest on other awards where the midpoint was to be taken, interest on an award for injury to feelings should normally be from the date of the discriminatory act. That must be taken to allow for the fact that injury to feelings is not a one-off event but something which will often persist over a period of time.*
>
> *In the present case, it was open to the tribunal to decline to find that serious injustice would be caused by adhering to the normal approach, and the EAT was not justified in interfering with the award.*

Interest therefore can be awarded at the discretion of the Employment Tribunal for acts of harassment, payable for the whole period for injury to feelings and for half the period for other elements of the compensatory award.

2.9 Recommendation

An Employment Tribunal may make a recommendation to the Employer if the Employer is found to be vicariously liable for discrimination.

Section 124 (2) (c) of the Equality Act 2010 grants the Employment Tribunal the power to make a recommendation. Section 124 (3) of the Equality Act 2010 specifies that the recommendation is appropriate if it recommends that the employer takes specified steps to reduce or obviate the adverse effect on the Claimant of any matter to which the proceedings relate.

A failure to implement a recommendation within the specified period without reasonable excuse can lead to an increase in the amount of compensation to be paid under section 124 (7) (b). The onus is on the Employer to prove that they have a reasonable excuse.

Recommendations can be and are made in harassment cases. An Employment Tribunal may recommend that an Employer introduce a Policy or Procedure to deal with harassment cases and to train employees on what harassment amounts to. Such a recommendation would reduce or obviate the adverse effect of harassment by instituting a measure that might prevent a repetition of the harassment. However such a recommendation could only be made if the employee has not left employment. If the employee has left employment then any training or introduction of policies or procedures would not obviate or reduce any adverse effects as the employee would not be affected as they would not be in employment.

2.10 Liability to pay

In **Sivanandan and others v Hackney London Borough Council** [2013] **2 All ER 940** the Claimant was awarded in excess of £421,455.00 for discrimination by way of victimisation. All bar £1905.41 of the award was payable by the Council with the balance of £1905.41 payable by one of the individual discriminators. The Council appealed the basis of apportionment of the award and whether liability was joint and several. The Court of Appeal held:

> *The damage suffered by the claimant in consequence of victimisation in the treatment of her two job applications had been indivisible, which had meant that, as against the claimant, no single tortfeasor had been liable only for consequences peculiar to his acts. Each had been jointly liable to the claimant for the full amount of the damage suffered by her. The indivisible character of the damage for which the authority and other respondents had been jointly liable had not been altered by the tribunal's error of law in purporting to apportion the liability of W to the claimant*

Joint and several liability for awards are a timely reminder for discriminators or harassers who work in small organisations who may go into administration leaving the individual discriminator or harasser liable for the employer's part of the award.

3. Taxation and Recoupment

The object of compensation is to put the same position as if the discrimination had not happened. The effect of this is that awards of compensation are made on a net of income tax and national insurance deductions basis.

Therefore if an employee earned £500.00 net per week or £750.00 gross a compensatory award would be paid tax free for loss of earnings up to £30,000.00. £30,000.00 is the tax-free allowance on termination. Sums awarded in excess of £30,000.00 as compensation for loss of earnings would be grossed up and taxed. Any award in excess of £30,000.00 would see the employer pay £750.00 per week of lost earnings and the employee receive £500.00 net of deductions.

Injury to feelings awards are taxable unless the award has a personal injury element to it thereby falling into the middle or upper band when it can be paid tax free.

Any part of the award that covers a period of time where the Claimant has received state benefit will make that state benefit repayable. The procedure for repayment is that the Employment Tribunal issues a recoupment notice to the employer which requires the employer to recoup a prescribed amount of money from the compensatory award and remit the prescribed amount to the Department of Work and Pensions.

4. Costs

Employment Tribunal hearings are non-contentious business. Costs do not follow the event. Each party ordinarily bears their own costs whether the claim is upheld or dismissed. The Employment Tribunal does have limited powers to award costs.

Those powers are contained at Schedule One in the Employment Tribunals (Constitution and Rules of Procedure) Regulations 2013. Rules 75 and 76 set out what can be ordered and in what circumstances.

The circumstances in which a costs order can be made are at Rule 76 where a party or their representative has acted vexatiously, abusively, disruptively, or otherwise unreasonably in the bringing or conduct of proceedings. Alternatively if either in bringing or defending the claim where either the claim or defence has no reasonable prospects of success.

Costs are a relatively rare event but one Claimants should be aware of. Whilst very few complaints of harassment are made up or fabricated, a Claimant will run the risks of a costs order if they do make up a claim.

5. Enforcement

Awards are payable within a set number of days, 14 days from the date the judgment was sent to the parties, after which interest of 8% is payable. If a person (employer or individual) fails to pay the award within the prescribed period then there is a fast track procedure for enforcement involving High Court enforcement officers.

6. Summary

An act of harassment is a statutory tort. A claimant can bring a claim against the tortfeasor and their employer. The tort has to have happened during the course of employment. Course of employment has been given a wide meaning and the Equality Act 2010 specifically outlaws harassment following employment if there is a causal connection between the harassment and former employment.

Whilst claims have to be brought within 3 months of the last act of harassment complained of Employment Tribunals are given a just and equitable discretion to extend time.

Employment Tribunals have power to award compensation for losses flowing from the tortious act. Compensation is not fettered by a cap it can be the full amount of the losses said to be suffered and claimed. The usual loss claimed is for loss of salary if the harassment results in a loss of job and income. The loss could be the difference between usual pay and sick pay, if the harassment has caused a period of illness and absence from work.

Furthermore Employment Tribunals can make an award for injury to feelings as well as any personal injury suffered as a result of the tortious act. An Employment Tribunal can also make a recommendation.

The Employment Tribunal's primary role is to make findings as to whether harassment has taken place. If it finds that harassment has taken place then the Employment Tribunal must make a declaration to that effect. That declaration is usually the most important part of the proceedings from the Claimant's point of view.

CHAPTER FOUR

HARASSMENT AND BULLYING OUTSIDE OF THE EQUALITY ACT 2010

In this Chapter we will be examining what sorts of bullying and harassing behaviour may be unlawful that has not been specifically outlawed by the Equality Act 2010. We will cast our net wide to see how laws not specifically aimed at the workplace can impact in the workplace. It will be taken as understood that actions that are crimes outside the workplace will also be criminal inside the workplace. It goes without saying that sexually assaulting a worker or employee or physically attacking causing grievous bodily harm will be criminal acts.

As we have seen the Equality Act 2010 specifically covers prohibited conduct during employment and has a definition of harassment. That definition of harassment encompasses intentional harassment as well as behaviour that leaves a victim feeling harassed without that being the intent of the perpetrator.

However there are other laws in place that protect UK citizens from being subject to harassment or oppressive and unreasonable conduct that impacts on them as individuals and leaves them feeling bullied.

Put another way there are laws in place that set the parameters of personal space and do not permit encroachment in defined ways into that personal space. Those laws if violated will render the perpetrator either civilly liable – liable for compensation for loss, or criminally liable, facing a criminal charge in the criminal courts. Those laws do not stop at the front door of the workplace and apply in and outside of work. We will not look at crimes of physical violence or sexual crimes.

We will look at four specific areas:

1. Right of privacy.

2. Data Rights. The General Data Protection Regulations 2018 set out the boundaries in which individual's personal data can be used and provide for remedies for data subjects for misuse of their data.

3. Right to truthful statements. Laws on defamation, libel, negligent misstatement also forbid untrue statements to be made about individuals. Making defamatory statements about a colleague will be a tort, rendering the tortfeasor liable for the loss caused by the tort.

4. The Protection from Harassment Act 2008 makes harassment a civil and criminal offence in defined circumstances.

We will look at all those rights and how they may impact on the workplace.

1. Right of Privacy

Citizens of the UK have certain freedoms. Some of those freedoms have been codified as enforceable legal rights. The Human Rights Act 1998 [HRA] which incorporates into UK Law the European Convention on Human Rights gives all UK citizens certain positive rights. Individuals cannot be subject to behaviour that encroaches on those rights.

A key positive right is at Article 8 of the HRA. Article 8 gives the right to respect for a private life. Article 8 is expressed in this way:

i. *Everyone has the right to respect for his private and family life, his home and his correspondence.*

ii. *There shall be no interference by a public authority with the exercise of this right except such as is in accordance with the law*

> *and is necessary in a democratic society in the interests of national security, public safety or the economic well-being of the country, for the prevention of disorder or crime, for the protection of health or morals, or for the protection of the rights and freedoms of others.*

In any issue before the courts the courts have to take into account whether there are issues under the HRA in play, whether fundamental rights given to every citizen have been transgressed.

The leading case on the right to privacy which touches on the Article 8 right to respect for the private life under the HRA is Campbell v Mirror Group Newspapers Limited [2004] UKHL 22.

The facts of the case relate to the Daily Mirror running a story and showing pictures of supermodel, Naomi Campbell, leaving a narcotics anonymous meeting.

The Court had to determine whether the following facts which were published were in breach of privacy:

i. the fact of Miss Campbell's drug addiction;

ii. the fact that she was receiving treatment;

iii. the fact that she was receiving treatment at Narcotics Anonymous;

iv. the details of the treatment – how long she had been attending meetings, how often she went, how she was treated within the sessions themselves, the extent of her commitment, and the nature of her entrance on the specific occasion; and

v. the visual portrayal of her leaving a specific meeting with other addicts.

Ms Campbell brought a claim for breach of confidence under the Data Protection Act 1998. A breach of confidence claim is in essence a claim alleging misuse of private information. Ms Campbell won her claim at first instance and was awarded £2,500.00 in damages. The damages were low as Ms Campbell was someone who the court found had courted publicity and had also been untruthful in public about whether she had taken illicit drugs.

The Daily Mirror lodged an appeal against the ruling and the case eventually ended up in the Supreme Court's predecessor, the House of Lords.

The House of Lords characterised a breach of confidence as an invasion of privacy claim and suggested that an unwarranted strip search could amount to giving rise to a claim in breach of confidence.

Whilst a claim in breach of confidence is a common law claim, the House of Lords noted that rights under the Human Rights Act 1998 were in play – namely right to respect for a private life [Article 8] and freedom of expression [Article 10]. The House of Lords stated:

> *The time has come to recognise that the values enshrined in articles 8 and 10 are now part of the cause of action for breach of confidence*

and

> *It is sufficient to recognise that the values underlying articles 8 and 10 are not confined to disputes between individuals and public authorities.*

The House of Lords held by a 3 to 2 majority that publishing facts 3 to 5 above did amount to a breach of confidentiality and an invasion of privacy.

The cases on privacy allow the Courts to adjudicate on whether an individual or organisation have overstepped the mark in intrusion into a private life. The concept was best explained in the case involving the wedding photos of Catherine Zeta-Jones and Michael Douglas, where

Michael Douglas sued OK magazine for publishing covertly taken photos of the wedding ceremony and reception. A rival publication to OK had exclusive rights to the wedding photos.

The Court of Appeal stated:

> *Lord Hoffmann identified two developments of the law of confidence. The first was the recognition of the artificiality of distinguishing between confidential information obtained through a violation of a confidential relationship and similar information obtained in some other way. The second was the acceptance, under human rights instruments such as Article 8 of the Convention, of the privacy of personal information as something worthy of protection in its own right. As to the latter there was no logical ground for affording a person less protection against a private individual than against the state. In the result (paragraph 51):*
>
> *"Instead of the cause of action being based upon the duty of good faith applicable to confidential personal information and trade secrets alike, it focuses upon the protection of human autonomy and dignity – the right to control the dissemination of information about one's private life and the right to the esteem and respect of other people.*

The law relating to privacy has developed in such a way as to protect human autonomy and dignity with the concomitant right to control the dissemination of information about one's private life and the right to the esteem and respect of other people towards an individual's private life.

A recent case involving Article 8 arguably extended the ambit of privacy further into professional reputation.

In the case of **Denisov v Ukraine** which was before the European Court of Human Rights under reference 76639/11, a claim was brought by a Judge from Ukraine who was dismissed by the state.

The judge complained under Article 6 (right to a fair trial) and Article 8 (the right to respect for his private life). The Judge argued that his Article 8 right had been infringed and that being dismissed had damaged his reputation. The ECHR stated:

> *General principles*
>
> *(i) "Private life" as a broad term*
>
> *95. The concept of "private life" is a broad term not susceptible to exhaustive definition. It covers the physical and psychological integrity of a person. It can therefore embrace multiple aspects of the person's physical and social identity. Article 8 protects in addition a right to personal development, and the right to establish and develop relationships with other human beings and the outside world (see S. and Marper v. the United Kingdom [GC], nos. 30562/04 and 30566/04, § 66, ECHR 2008; Gillberg, cited above, § 66; and Barbulescu v. Romania [GC], no. 61496/08, § 70, ECHR 2017 (extracts), with further references therein).*
>
> *96. Therefore, it would be too restrictive to limit the notion of "private life" to an "inner circle" in which the individual may live his own personal life as he chooses and to exclude therefrom entirely the outside world not encompassed within that circle (see Fernández Martínez, cited above, § 109).*
>
> *(ii) Right to respect for reputation*
>
> *97. Alongside this development in the case-law, the Court has been called upon to determine whether the notion of "private life" should cover a right to respect for reputation, which is not expressly mentioned in Article 8. In Pfeifer v. Austria (no. 12556/03, § 35, 15 November 2007) the Court, having regard to its case-law, found that a person's reputation, even if that person was criticised in the context of a public debate, formed part of his or her personal identity and psychological*

integrity and therefore also fell within the scope of his or her "private life".

The ECHR reviewed the authorities and saw that Article 8 could be engaged in two ways – either because the reason for dismissal encroaches on an individual's private life, dismissal for example because of homosexuality, or because the consequences of dismissal knock into an individual's private life.

Their summary was:

> *Conclusions: the scope of Article 8 in employment-related disputes*
>
> *115. The Court concludes from the above case-law that employment-related disputes are not per se excluded from the scope of "private life" within the meaning of Article 8 of the Convention. There are some typical aspects of private life which may be affected in such disputes by dismissal, demotion, non-admission to a profession or other similarly unfavourable measures. These aspects include (i) the applicant's "inner circle", (ii) the applicant's opportunity to establish and develop relationships with others, and (iii) the applicant's social and professional reputation. There are two ways in which a private-life issue would usually arise in such a dispute: either because of the underlying reasons for the impugned measure (in that event the Court employs the reason-based approach) or – in certain cases – because of the consequences for private life (in that event the Court employs the consequence-based approach).*
>
> *116. If the consequence-based approach is at stake, the threshold of severity with respect to all the above-mentioned aspects assumes crucial importance. It is for the applicant to show convincingly that the threshold was attained in his or her case. The applicant has to present evidence substantiating consequences of the impugned measure. The Court will only accept that Article 8 is applicable where these consequences are very serious and affect his or her private life to a very significant degree.*

> *117. The Court has established criteria for assessing the severity or seriousness of alleged violations in different regulatory contexts. An applicant's suffering is to be assessed by comparing his or her life before and after the measure in question. The Court further considers that in determining the seriousness of the consequences in employment-related cases it is appropriate to assess the subjective perceptions claimed by the applicant against the background of the objective circumstances existing in the particular case. This analysis would have to cover both the material and the non-material impact of the alleged measure. However, it remains for the applicant to define and substantiate the nature and extent of his or her suffering, which should have a causal connection with the impugned measure. Having regard to the rule of exhaustion of domestic remedies, the essential elements of such allegations must be sufficiently raised before the domestic authorities dealing with the matter.*

In the case of **Barbelsecu v Romania** the ECHR held that the claimant, an employee, had his right to privacy breached under Article 8 when his employer monitored and read a professional instant messaging account that his employer had set up. In particular the right of privacy for private life and correspondence was breached because the employer had failed to notify the employee that his instant messaging account would be monitored and his instant messages, some of which were private in content, would be read.

We can see then that individuals have the right to respect for a private life and a family life. The Courts will intervene if that right is intruded on without good reason.

The right to a private life can in limited circumstances impact on employment decisions where an employer's actions damage professional standing and reputation.

In the case of Spadijer v Montenegro, a prison guard reported several males' colleagues for inappropriate conduct involving female prisoners on New Year's Eve. She faced retaliation for her report such as verbal abuse, property damage and harassment at work. Despite her complaints, the prison officials took insufficient action, dismissing her claims and stating that surveillance cameras evidencing these crimes were not function. The Claimant was told that the cameras were functional and could have collaborated with her claim. In Montenegrin law, her claim did not meet the requirements of bullying. The law for bullying stated that incidents had to be weekly over six months.

The case was sent to the European Court of Human Rights which found that the Respondent had violated the Claimant's Article 8 rights. The court emphasises that the prison had failed to protect her rights, especially because harassment appeared to be linked to her whistleblowing activities.

2. Data Rights

As we have seen above Employers need to be mindful about intruding too far into an employee's personal and private life. Furthermore an employer needs to handle with care any confidential information relating to any employee's personal or family life, for example issues relating to health or sexuality. Claims alleging breach of privacy are also coupled in many cases, for example Campbell and Douglas cases, with a claim under the GDPR or predecessor legislation. The claim is put that not only was privacy invaded but also that data protection rights of the data subject were breached.

Whilst Employment Tribunals are notoriously slow to say that HRA rights are engaged, employers do need to be aware that such rights exist and need to weigh any intrusion into an employee's private life against the need to intrude. Covert surveillance is one area that some employers use in certain limited circumstances, usually where an employee is off sick and believed to be swinging the lead, that may give rise to an allegation that privacy has been invaded.

A case I conducted for an employer at Huntingdon Employment Tribunal which involved the use of data from a vehicle tracker was not seen to be an intrusion into private life as the employee knew that trackers had been installed in his work's van. The tracker data did show that the employee's van was regularly parked outside during work time for 2 to 3 hours at a time at an address that was not his home address.

If an organisation has data about an individual then that individual is a data subject under the General Data Processing Regulations [GDPR]. Employers are data controllers under the GDPR. Larger employers have to employ a nominated person with a specific remit to be responsible for data in the organisation.

Every data subject has the right to have their data processed in accordance with the regulations. Employers have to process data subject's data in accordance with the GDPR. The data subject's consent to process the data is often required.

Throughout the lifecycle of an employee, an employer may be privy to confidential information about the employee. An employer may store data about an employee's sexuality, age, marital status, health, criminal record or credit record or disciplinary history.

That data is confidential and should not be readily shared by the employer without either the consent of the data subject or without a very good reason with such a reason being permissible under GDPR.

Sharing confidential data about an employee in breach of the GDPR will leave the employee with the right of redress in the courts.

I brought a claim for an employee in the County Court where her data rights had been breached. The data transgression was when a Director had informed a customer via email that that employee was off sick with stress and that she was also subject to a disciplinary meeting. Such data, the fact and nature of sickness as well as being subject to a disciplinary, was personal data of the data subject's and she had not consented to that data being shared with a customer. Furthermore there was no permissible reason under the GDPR to share that data with a third party without the data subject's consent. Idle gossip did not constitute a good reason. The result was a four-figure settlement which the employer agreed to very much with gritted teeth,

A more recent and widely publicised case was Morrison's Supermarkets data breach. An IT Audit Manager, a Mr Skelton, put 99,000 employees' personal payroll data on an USB memory stick and then sold the data to the dark web. Mr Skelton then wrote to three national newspapers anonymously and gave them links to where the data was stored on the dark web. Mr Skelton was subsequently charged, convicted and imprisoned with an 8-year sentence. Over 5,000 employees then brought claims for damages against Morrisons for breach of their data rights.

Morrisons argued that as Mr Skelton put the data on the dark web from home using his own equipment on a Sunday then there was no close connection between the criminal acts of Mr Skelton and Morrisons employment of him to render Morrisons vicariously liable. Both the High Court and Court of Appeal disagreed on that point but did agree that Mr Skelton at the time of the offence was the data controller. There was a chain of events starting and ending with Morrisons employment of Mr Skelton which rendered them vicariously liable for Mr Skelton's actions. In particular the Courts gave a purposive approach to interpretation of the Data Protection Act 1998 to ensure that the purpose of data protection law. And the purpose of the law was:

> *namely the protection of privacy and the provision of an effective remedy for its infringement (including by an employee of limited means), rather than their curtailment.*

A breach of GDPR may be sufficiently serious to allow the employee to resign and claim the breach amounts to a repudiation of the contract and give rise to a claim for constructive unfair dismissal.

Breach of GDPR by a data controller can cause distress and upset to a data subject. Employers need to take steps to protect data subjects' rights to have their data processed in accordance with the law.

3. Right to truthful statements

Every individual in the UK has the right of redress if untrue and harmful statements are made against them. Those rights emanate from different sources.

One source is the common law, principles that have been extracted over the years from cases that have come before the court.

The common law in relation to contracts has developed the idea that contracts have implied terms in them if certain conditions are met.

Similarly under the common law an employer owes third parties a duty of care in relation to actions and omissions that affect that third party.

One area where the common law has been engaged is in the area of references. The leading case is Spring v. Guardian Assurance plc and others [1994] IRLR 460 which went to the House of Lords. In that case a Mr Spring lost out on a job because of a reference given to him by his former employer, part of the Guardian Assurance Group.

The House of Lords held that there was an implied contractual right to write a reference with skill and care as well as a duty of care to both the subject of the reference and the recipient. If a reference was written in breach of the duty of care then the reference giver could be liable to the subject of the reference if economic loss flowed from the negligence. Alternatively the reference giver could be liable for any economic loss of the recipient if relying on a negligent reference to employ someone unsuitable who then causes economic loss to the recipient.

We see many clients who have had their employment prospects and wellbeing adversely affected by negative references. A poorly prepared and negligent reference can leave a former employee to feel bullied and humiliated.

Similarly oral and written statements made in the workplace are subject to the law of defamation, malicious falsehood and libel.

Whilst a detailed examination of these laws is outside the remit of this book employers do need a base understanding of the law to ensure that communications are professional and fact based.

The Defamation Act 2012 has codified the law in relation to Defamation. In summary if an untrue statement is published that causes serious harm to the subject matter of the statement then that may give rise to a claim for damages, unless there is a statutory defence available.

Defamation and libel claims are a high-risk activity. The losing party has to pay the winning party's costs ordinarily. Costs, even with budgeting processes in place, can easily reach six figures. Defamation cases are a rare event in the workplace for the obvious reason that most employees cannot afford to take the risk. The defamation sabre is often rattled by a disgruntled employee but that rattled sabre rarely leads to a claim being issued.

We have recently acted for an employee sued for defamation by her employer. The claim centred on complaints made the employee to a regulator, the CQC, that the employer had a number of health risks present at his premises. The claim was struck out as the statements made to the regulator were true, they were in any event covered by privilege, and lastly there was no serious harm caused to the employer by the statements that were made. The CQC followed up the statements but took no further action.

The case of **Singh v Weayou** was a defamation claim brought by a Mr Singh a mental health nurse against a colleague a Mr Weayou, a health care assistant. Mr Weayou had complained via email to HR that he had been subjected to sexual harassment and then an alleged campaign after those advances were resisted to push her out of her employment.

The High Court held that the published words were untrue and had caused serious harm to Mr Singh and furthermore that they amounted to malicious falsehood and Mr Weayou did not hold an honest belief in the truth of the allegations he had made. Mr Singh was awarded over £25,000.00 in damages for the losses he had suffered, including injury to feelings.

Employers need to ensure that statements made about their employees or ex-employees are fact based, truthful and if expressing an opinion for that opinion to have facts to support it and be honestly held.

4. Harassment under Protection from Harassment Act 1997

The Protection from Harassment Act 1997 outlaws harassing conduct.

Harassment is not well defined but section1 of the Act defines the unlawfulness as:

> '(1) *A person must not pursue a course of conduct—(a) which amounts to harassment of another, and (b) which he knows or ought to know amounts to harassment of the other.*
>
> *(2) For the purposes of this section, the person whose course of conduct is in question ought to know that it amounts to harassment of another if a reasonable person in possession of the same information would think the course of conduct amounted to harassment of the other.*'

Section 7 (3) of the Act further qualifies that by saying that the course of conduct must happen at least two occasions. Furthermore an act of harassment whilst not defined will be behaviour that causes anxiety and distress at section 1 (3).

The Act imposes civil as well as criminal liability and applies everywhere including workplaces. A defendant has a defence if the course of conduct was for the purpose of preventing or detecting a crime. The scope of that defence is examined in detail in Hayes V Willoughby

[2013] 2 All ER 405. The defence is not limited to regulatory bodies or the police but to private individuals.

There have been a number of cases brought under the Protection from Harassment Act 1997 by employees or former employees relating to alleged acts of harassment that took place in the workplace. Such claims should be brought within 3 years of the date the harassment ceased.

The leading case is **Majrowoski v Guys' and St Thomas's NHS Trust**. That case ended up in the House of Lords.

The facts as put in the Lords' judgement were put as follows:

> *The harassment in this case concerns two employees of Guy's and St Thomas's NHS Trust (the trust). In November 1998 the trust employed William Majrowski as a clinical auditor co-ordinator. His departmental manager was Mrs Sandra Freeman. Mr Majrowski was not happy with the way she treated him. He claimed she bullied and intimidated him. She was, he said, rude and abusive to him in front of other staff. She was excessively critical of his time-keeping and work. She imposed unrealistic performance targets for him and threatened him with disciplinary action if he failed to meet them. She isolated him by refusing to talk to him. This treatment, he said, was fuelled by homophobia: he is a gay man.*

Mr Majrowski brought a complaint of harassment internally at the Trust and the Trust found that he had been harassed. Mr Majrowski subsequently lost his job for reasons unrelated to the harassment and sometime later brought a claim for damages against his employer for damages for being harassed by Ms Freeman, an employee of the Trust.

The Trust denied that they could be vicariously liable for unlawful acts of its employees and the claim was dismissed summarily in first instance. Mr Majrowski appealed and the Court of Appeal held by 2 to 1 that in principle the Trust could be vicariously liable for unlawful acts of its employees and it was sent for trial as to whether harassment had in fact taken place. The Trust appealed to the House of Lords. The House of Lords dismissed the appeal and found that the Trust and any employer could be vicariously liable for acts of harassment committed by an employee during the course of their employment:

> *Vicarious liability is a common law principle of strict, no-fault liability. Under this principle a blameless employer is liable for a wrong committed by his employee while the latter is about his employer's business. The time-honoured phrase is 'while acting in the course of his employment'. It is thus a form of secondary liability. The primary liability is that of the employee who committed the wrong... This principle of vicarious liability is at odds with the general approach of the common law. Normally common law wrongs, or torts, comprise particular types of conduct regarded by the common law as blameworthy. In respect of these wrongs the common law imposes liability on the wrongdoer himself. The general approach is that a person is liable only for his own acts.*

The Majrowski case established that an employer could be on the hook and liable for any unlawful acts of harassment under the Protection from Harassment Act 1997 committed by one of their employees during the course of their employment. Baroness Hale stressed in the judgment that whether or acts amounted to acts of harassment depended on context and were fact sensitive:

> *'A great deal is left to the wisdom of the courts to draw sensible lines between the ordinary banter and badinage of life and genuinely offensive and unacceptable behaviour.'*

Since Majrowski a number of cases have been brought under the Protection from Harassment Act 1997 involving alleged harassment at work have reached courts. Going through those cases we can extract the following principles:

In Green v DB Services Limited discussed in Chapter one, the Judge found that not only did the conduct amount to bullying and the employer was vicariously liable in negligence for allowing the bullying to take place, the Judge also found that the bullying breached the Protection from Harassment Act 1997 observing:

> *To constitute harassment within the meaning of the Act, there must have been conduct: (a) occurring on at least two occasions, (b) targeted at the claimant, (c) calculated in an objective sense to cause distress, and (d) which is objectively judged to be oppressive and unreasonable.*

In **Sunderland City Council v Conn** [2007] **EWCA Civ 1492** the trial judge found that a foreman, Mr Dryden, employed by the Council had committed acts of harassment against a paver whom he supervised. Whilst five acts of harassment had been alleged by Mr Conn, only two had been proven firstly when Mr Dryden had asked Mr Conn and two other colleagues of the names of colleagues who had left site early. When no names were forthcoming Mr Dryden had threatened to smash the windows of the cabin. The second allegation that was upheld was that Mr Conn had questioned Mr Dryden as to why he was giving Mr Conn the silent treatment. Mr Dryden then said he would only talk to Mr Conn about work and then had lost his temper and threatened to give Mr Conn a hiding if it meant he, Mr Dryden, would be dismissed for that. The Council appealed. The Court of Appeal allowed the appeal and held that the facts found did not amount harassment. They held that:

> *According to the House of Lords in Majrowksi v Guy's and St Thomas's NHS Trust, to cross the boundary from the regrettable to the unacceptable, the gravity of the misconduct must be of an order which would sustain criminal liability under s.2 of the 1997 Act.*

And later in the judgement:

> *What crosses the boundary between unattractive and even unreasonable conduct and conduct that is oppressive and unacceptable may well depend on the context in which the conduct occurs. What might not be harassment on the factory floor and in the barrack room might well be harassment in the hospital ward and vice versa. The touchstone for recognising what is not harassment for the purposes of ss.1 and 3 will be whether the conduct is of such gravity as to justify the sanctions of the criminal law…and the first proven incident did not cross the boundary into conduct which could be said to be unlawful. The incident was no doubt unpleasant, so far as Mr Conn was concerned. However, no threat of violence had been made; only a threat to damage property. The remarks had been addressed to three people, not just to Mr Conn, and although Mr Conn had been agitated, neither of the other two colleagues had been troubled by it. It was the sort of bad-tempered conduct which, although unpleasant, came well below the line of that which justified a criminal sanction. It followed that the recorder had been wrong to find that were two incidents sufficient to amount to a course of conduct. The recorder's judgment that the council were vicariously liable for harassment would be set aside.*

Lord Justice Ward went further and said:

> *I agree with both judgments given by my Lords. I am tempted only to add: what on earth is the world coming to if conduct of the kind that occurred in the third incident can be thought to be an act of harassment, potentially liable to giving rise to criminal proceedings punishable with imprisonment for a term not exceeding six months, and to a claim for damages for anxiety and financial loss? It falls so far short below the threshold that we are in my judgment fully entitled to interfere with the judgment of the recorder, even though he had the benefit of seeing the witnesses and judging the facts as they appeared before him. The conduct here does not come close to harassment and I would therefore allow the appeal, set aside his order, and enter judgment: dismiss the claim of the claimant for damages in its entirely.*

In Dowson and others v the Chief Constable of Northumberland *[2010] EWHC 2612 (QB)* the Claimants, Police officers brought claims of harassment about the conduct of their superior, a DCI Pallas, for which they alleged that the defendant the Chief Constable was vicariously liable. The allegations were many and detailed but were summarised by the trial judge as:

> *8. The six Claimants claim that from the moment he arrived in July 2002, DCI Pallas adopted a hostile and critical attitude, that he harassed each of them on the basis that they were part of Mr Dowson's 'team' or 'clique' and that this harassment continued until each of them had left CTN by July 2003.*
>
> *9. Although it will be necessary to consider 30 detailed allegations of harassment it is convenient to summarise the general nature of the allegations at this stage.*
>
> *10. Some complaints are about instructions which required them to act contrary to the law or incompatibly with the standards of behaviour expected of a member of the Force. There are other complaints that DCI Pallas covered up his own shortcomings by blaming the Claimants for his own failings; and in doing so accused the Claimants of lying or failing in their duty. There are also complaints of vulgar abuse, particularly in front of subordinates. There are other complaints of unjustified and otherwise demeaning criticisms made by DCI Pallas which were intended to undermine individual Claimants and which he would have known would be repeated to them. There are further complaints that that the Claimants suffered further consequences of his harassment in the treatment of their formal complaints of bullying and harassment against him under the Northumbria Force Grievance Procedure. It is also alleged that these complaints were rejected and that the Claimants were removed from CTN because senior Officers accepted DCI Pallas's untruthful denials of misconduct.*

After a detailed review of the evidence and an assessment of the credibility of the witnesses the trial judge found that no harassment had taken place as the unique circumstances of the workplace had to be taken into account as well as the fact that DCI Pallas had not acted in an intentional way to cause stress and anxiety. The Judge found as follows:

> *The question is whether this conduct constituted harassment. I have concluded that it did not. This was a stressful working environment in which case-hardened officers were dealing with career-hardened criminals. Although this was more than simply a clash of personalities, it was not conduct which was calculated to cause distress and, although it was unacceptable, it was not oppressive in the sense described in the cases. It was not a tormenting by constant interference or intimidation. Rather it was a curt and dismissive attitude which was likely to have the effect, even if unintended, of undermining both Mr Dowson's own self-confidence and the esteem in which he was held by others.*

In Suttle v Walker a claim under the Protection from Harassment Act 1997 the Court found that Ms Walker had harassed the Claimant by setting up a Facebook group which had picked on and made untrue statements about the Claimant. The conduct amounted to cyber bullying and constituted harassment under the Act. In determining remedy the Judge, The Honourable Mr Justice Nicklin, stated as follows:

> *I consider that the following particular elements of the harassment, separate from the harassing element in the defamatory nature of the publications themselves, have an impact on the seriousness of the harassment and to the assessment of damages:*
>
> *a. The campaign was clearly and deliberately targeted by the Defendant at the Claimant via Facebook. The foreseeable response to it was vicious and frightening; it was calculated to (and did) whip up hatred for the Claimant and to put her in fear for her safety.*
>
> *b. The campaign was relentless over a period of three to four weeks and I am satisfied, on the evidence, that has had a lasting adverse effect on the Claimant.*

> *c. The use of a Facebook group was deliberately to recruit others to 'gang up' on the Claimant, whilst the Defendant and some of the commentators who chose to post comments on the page hid behind online anonymity. This is a hallmark of 'cyber bullying'. It is a particularly pernicious form of harassment because the victim may well feel constantly under siege and powerless to stop it.*

The Judge also stated that the Vento bands were relevant in determining damages for injury to feelings.

We can see therefore that employers employ individuals who have freestanding rights which apply within the workplace. Breach of those rights can leave the employee feeling distressed and bullied.

In the case of Birmingham City Council v Afsar and others [2019] EWHC, the council sought injunctions to restrict street protests and online abuse targeting a primary school's LGBT teaching. The main legal issue was whether such restrictions were lawful, given the protesters' rights to free speech and assembly under the European Convention on Human Rights. The court ruled that the Anti-social Behaviour, Crime and Policing Act 2014 allowed injunctions in this context, as the legislation was clear and did not exclude protests. While freedom of expression is important, it is not absolute, and the restrictions were deemed necessary and proportionate to prevent disorder and protect others' rights. However, no restrictions on social media activity were justified.

In the case of Collier and others v Bennett [2020] EWHC 1884, the claimants, C, R, and O, alleged they were defamed and harassed by a Twitter user under the pseudonym Harry Tuttle. They sought Norwich Pharmacal relief to identify the account holder and recover deleted tweets to support their claims. They suspected B, who controlled the account, was the author but B refused to confirm this, arguing the claimants' case was weak and unnecessary. The court held that C and R had demonstrated a valid defamation claim and the conditions for Norwich Pharmacal relief were met. It ruled that disclosure of the tweets and the account holder's identity was necessary and proportionate, rejecting B's defense.

Those rights are:

a. The right to privacy.

b. The right to have their data treated in accordance with their rights under the Data Protection legislation.

c. The rights to have statements made about them which are true and made in accordance with legal principles.

d. The right not to be harassed under the Protection from Harassment Act 1997.

Breach of those rights can leave the individual transgressor liable as well as their employer vicariously liable for the breach. Such liability will depend on the loss flowing from the breach but can be substantial if loss of health or income arise.

In the final chapter we will look at ways employers can mitigate the risks of harm arising from breaches of legal obligations owed to employees and breaches of their rights.

CHAPTER FIVE

PREVENTION OF, AND DEFENCES TO, HARASSMENT AND BULLYING CLAIMS

We have seen in chapter one that bullying behaviour can give rise to a claim for unfair dismissal as a repudiatory breach of contract by the employer. It can also give rise to a claim for negligence for personal injury.

We have seen in chapters two and three how the law of harassment in the workplace has evolved in the discrimination legislation culminating in harassment being a discrete act of discrimination.

The Equality Act 2010 sets out the what harassment is and what conduct is prohibited. The law on harassment under the Equality Act 2010 can leave the perpetrator individually liable as well as the employer vicariously liable. We have also seen that harassment claims give the employer the possibility of a statutory defence under the Equality Act 2010 of having taken all reasonably practicable steps to prevent harassment in the workplace. If an employer can make out the statutory defence then the individual perpetrator can be left holding the liability baby.

Finally we have seen in chapter four that employees as individual citizens have the rights not to have their privacy unlawfully invaded, their data unlawfully processed, and for what is written or communicated about them not to fall foul of the laws governing written and oral communications. We have also seen how the law makes harassing conduct unlawful under the Protection from Harassment Act 1997.

How then does the employer protect itself and defend itself from possible claims? That is a very large question indeed.

Firstly prevention is best. Whilst loss of a job and income is for many if not most employees or workers a situation that is recoverable usually within a short space of time, loss of health and or loss of confidence may take longer to recover from and for some employees or workers the damage to health or confidence or well-being may be permanent.

Inflicting damage on an employee's health, well-being, or confidence is not what any employer wants to do. So let's look at prevention. The best place to start with ensuring that an employee's or worker's health is not damaged in the workplace is to have robust health and safety processes in place. With the move away from manual work where physical injury may result, many office-based workplaces have greater risks of mental health injury rather than physical injury.

The HSE see culture as all important. If an organisation can engrain the right culture an organisation can prevent employees or workers from being injured in the workplace.

The airline sector has culture down to a fine art. The airline sector has processes in place, where lessons are learnt from near misses or from accidents' causes via the black box in every aeroplane. Safety first culture is so engrained that consequently flying in a plane is now one of the safest ways of travel.

Risks and hazards can be engineered out or mitigated to a large extent if the right processes and principles are in place. Process and principle need to be hand in hand. The principle is that employers need to ensure that their workplaces are healthy and safe. The processes should support and underpin the underlying principle.

The HSE recognise three major occupational health and safety systems or codified processes that are in use globally.

They are:

1. **HSG65**: this system has been developed by the HSE and is used extensively in the UK.

2. **OHSAS 18001:** has been developed in conjunction with the quality standard ISO 9000 series.

3. **ILO -OSH 2001:** has been developed by the International Labour Organisation [ILO] after an extensive study of many occupational health and safety management systems used across the world.

HSG65 was developed by HSE in 1991 and has been amended since then. Its focus is on continual improvement. As the system was developed by the HSE it is widely used in the UK. It is available as a free downloadable PDF from the HSE website.

The constituent parts of HSG65 are:

1. **A health and safety policy**: The policy should set out a systematic approach to risk assessment and sufficient resources have been allocated to protect the health, welfare, and safety of the workforce. Health and safety processes should be aligned with quality and continuous improvement processes.

2. **A well-defined health and safety organisation:** where there are shared values and beliefs at all levels of the organisation. Shared values and beliefs, or culture, is an essential component in an effective health and safety system. The organisation will have visibility on who is responsible for health and safety, who is accountable, as well as widespread involvement of the workforce in developing feedback mechanisms to enable continuous improvement in health and safety processes.

3. **A clear health and safety plan**: The plan should set and implement standards and procedures using an effective health and safety management system. The plan should use risk assessments to identify priorities and set objectives for controlling or eliminating hazards and reducing risks. This is particularly important following the October 2024 amendments. Employers should conduct and make a record of a risk assessment for risk of sexual harassment.

4. **The measurement of health and safety performance**: The monitoring should be proactive and reactive. Proactive in assessing the risks in premises, equipment, substances, people and procedures.

5. **Reviewing performance:** Reviews should be systematic. If there have been accidents or near misses then reviews should be conducted. Comparisons should be made internally as well as externally with other organisations within the sector. The risk assessment for sexual harassment should be kept under recorded review.

6. **Auditing:** An independent and structured audit process reviewing the operation of the health and safety policy and underlying processes. External audits may be more valuable than internal audits.

The four key characteristics of a successful occupational health and safety management system are:

1. **A positive health and safety culture**: That means leadership and commitment to health and safety, aa clear and communicated policy, adherence to high standards, identification of significant hazards, a detailed assessment of risks, clear consultation and communication processes, systems for monitoring health and safety, quick investigation of all incidents, prompt reporting and implementation of remedial measures.

2. **An involvement of all stakeholders**: That means internal stakeholders such as the management team, the workforce, the health and safety professionals as well as external stakeholders such as the insurance companies, regulators such as HSE, customers and any employer's organisations.

3. **An effective audit**: This is the final and most crucial part of the feedback loop. It seeks to establish whether appropriate processes and mechanisms are in place as well as effective risk control systems and workplace precautions are established and working.

4. **Continual improvement**: This process is essential. The best way of improving year in, year out is to implement the recommendations of reports, reviews and audits.

Health and safety has traditionally been associated with physical injury rather than mental injury. Slowly that emphasis has shifted. As the economy moves to a service and knowledge economy, employers and organisations will need to align their health and safety processes to manage the risks inherent in workplaces where the labour outputs are cerebral rather than physical and where the risks are as much to mental health as to physical health. The manufacturing industry is shrinking as a proportion of the economy meaning that the risk of physical injury to employees shrinks with it.

The incidence of factory type injuries such as losing a finger or a limb is reducing in line with the declining share in manufacturing. Whilst physical injuries such as back injuries caused by manual handling of files or eye injuries or damage caused by display screen equipment or repetitive strain injury caused by repetitive processes such as typing can take place in an office environment, risks of injuries of that type can be mitigated by adapting equipment or processes.

It is increasingly being recognised that excessive workloads against tight timelines can cause employees to feel unsupported and bullied and that those stressors can lead to a breakdown in health as was illustrated in

Walker and Northumberland Council case. Similarly it is also being recognised that negative behaviour of managers and supervisors can adversely affect health and well-being, as illustrated by the Majrowski case.

The Health and Safety Executive is taking a closer interest and involvement in mental injury and prevention of poor mental health caused by workplace practices. Many employers are now training up and designating employees as mental health first aiders.

If an organisation has well-honed health and safety practices in place, feedback loops will also be in place which will identify poor workplace practices like workload allocation or negative behaviour that could cause poor mental health. Organisations that have those feedback loops in place will be able to minimise those risks effectively.

Given that bullying and harassment is behavioural in nature, prevention is cultural. Culture is integral to a safe and healthy workplace.

Standards of behaviour should be set by the leadership team and those standards should be inculcated throughout the organisation. If there are instances of bullying or harassing behaviour revealed during a grievance process or highlighted by monitoring absences for stress, depression or anxiety then that feedback should be acted on.

It is recognised that behaviour may be unintentional but have the effect of leaving an employee feeling bullied. Therefore those with responsibility for supervising or managing employees should be trained in appropriate management styles and made aware of management styles and behaviour that can leave employees feeling bullied.

Ultimately bullying and harassment is not showing the recipient any respect. Respect and dignity for the individual should be a cornerstone value for every organisation.

Health and safety processes will put that cornerstone value into practice by ensuring that the workplace is as safe and healthy as it can be and ensuring that any risks and hazards are minimised and mitigated. Health and safety law firmly plants the responsibility for breaches of health and safety on those holding a director level position and in extreme cases breaches of health and safety law can be a criminal offence rendering those responsible for the failure liable to criminal prosecution.

Preventing invasions of privacy and other acts

Employers should have procedures in place to protect their employees' and workers' personal data. Those who hold management and supervisory positions should be trained in how to handle sensitive and personal data. Again respect is key.

Similarly managers and supervisors should be aware of the need for accurate and factually supported communications both internally and externally about other individuals. The workplace is not immune from the laws of defamation, malicious falsehood and libel. Publishing a falsehood that causes serious harm to an individual without justification will render the publisher liable.

Publication means more than writing in a newspaper or magazine it covers all forms of written communication including email and social media. Serious harm means harm to the individual's reputation. Organisations and their workforce should take care in their written and oral communications to ensure that such communications are factually accurate, supported by evidence and moderate in tone. Stick to those guidelines and there should be no difficulty.

Employers should have well developed and up to date policies on use of IT and Social Media. Furthermore employers should communicate their right to monitor and read email and instant messaging accounts that have been set up by the employer.

How does an employer prevent harassment?

Whilst bullying has not been precisely defined as a wrong in employment law, the cases show that bullying can be grounds for constructive dismissal and negligence a claim for damages if losses flow from the bullying such as ill health.

Harassment does have a definition both in the Equality Act 2010 and the Protection from Harassment Act 1997 [PFH].

The Equality Act 2010 gives employers a statutory defence as does the POH to a limited extent if the conduct is for the prevention or detection of criminal acts. The hurdle for claims under the Protection from Harassment Act 1997 is a high one, the acts of harassment alleged have to have a quality of criminal conduct. Unreasonable conduct won't meet the definition. Offensive and bullying behaviour that is intended to harm and upset the recipient may well meet the definition under the PFH 1997.

Health and Safety law places an emphasis on processes and an organisational culture that supports and resources a healthy and safe workplace. Harassment law places an emphasis on reasonably practicable steps and those reasonably practicable steps are having a policy in place and procedures to support the policy and training and awareness programmes to ensure that all of the workplace is aware of what the appropriate standards of behaviour and conduct are as well as what sanctions are there for failing to adhere to those standards of behaviour. However policy, process and procedure are insufficient unless the culture of an organisation is positive. Or put another way toxic workplaces won't prevent harassment or bullying simply by having policies and procedures in place. It comes down to how people within the workplace treat one another. If we treat one another in a way that they would like to be treated then those workplaces won't often have to reach for their policies and procedures to deal with any issue as those issues won't arise regularly.

To contextualise the importance of work in one's life, there are usually three key relationships in a person's life.

1. Family.

2. Friends.

3. Work.

The foundation block of all three relationships is trust. Without trust there is no relationship. When a relationship breaks down there is often a substantial impact on the parties. HR practitioners know that when an employee is going through a divorce or separation there is quite often a knock-on effect on the employee and their performance may be adversely affected.

Whilst policies and procedures have a critical place in any organisation, policies and procedures are, or should be, a fallback position. If you are having to look to the policies or procedures for guidance this suggests there is a problem.

Stopping bullying and harassment in the workplace is primarily one of establishing and ensuring that the workplace has a culture where harassment and bullying behaviour is not acceptable. Culture is defined as a set of shared assumptions. The assumption should be that employees and workers should be able to work in a workplace that is free from harassment.

The leaders in any organisation set the tone, set the business standards of behaviour, set the targets and operational objectives. The fish rots from the head down. The ultimate and best defence is prevention. Prevention is best for the organisation, best for the workforce and best for meeting the organisation's objectives. Poor health behaviours like smoking, drinking, excessive weight will lead to a bigger risk of poor outcomes for those indulging. Similarly an organisation with poor behavioural standards is likely to be not only at risk of poor organisational outcomes like reduced productivity and increased absence.

The leadership team need to be trusted not only to behave in a way that is consistent with the culture of the organisation but also should be trusted to deal with any issues that arise, any complaints that arise, any grievances that are lodged in a way that is consistent with the organisation's culture.

If we look back at the reported cases we find all too often that an organisation has either turned a blind eye to harassment that is alleged to have taken place – for example in Tower Boot v Jones – or has actively set poor behavioural standards – for example in Insitsu Cleaning Limited v Head. Alternatively when management are tasked with dealing with a complaint of harassment management have failed to deal with the complaint appropriately, thereby aggravating the original offence and catapulting the issue that could have been resolved internally into an external legal forum, with all the reputational risk that entails. An example of an organisation failing to deal with a complaint of bullying or harassment appropriately is Green v DB Services.

Over the years I have given many in-house talks and training sessions to organisations throughout the UK. When giving such talks I am often faced with attendees who would rather not be there and have been asked to attend by HR. The body language of the attendees reminded me of the body language and demeanour, including my own, of attendees on a driver awareness course who are attending in lieu of accepting driving points on their licence. A lot of folded arms, rolled eyes, and barely stifled yawns. The initial mindset of many groups was that such sessions are "politically correct" and that they are being required to attend as part of training for compliance purposes – to protect the organisation from risk.

However senior management teams of organisations, whether they are in the private sector or public sector, are all tasked with the same thing. The purpose of management is to use the resources at their disposal in a productive way. Having a workplace free from bullying and harassment sets the environment for employees and workers to do their job in a productive way. Bullying and harassment set a negative environment. Negative environments do not allow a workforce to give their best. Ultimately if a workplace environment allows bullying and harassment a negative feedback loop sets in which impacts on staff retention and reputation.

The hard data shows that organisations that have the best records for equal opportunities, that tackle discrimination head on and early have the best track record for growth. Hard-headed leaders realise that there is a strong business case for having a friendly and positive workplace. Over the years I have seen the decline in the old school of management. Old school managers or Directors who rule their function or organisation with a rod of iron, who shout, bang their fists on the table and assert their authority through a climate of fear are a dying breed. Most organisations are looking for senior managers and directors to have softer skills and emotional intelligence.

An obvious point to make is that a senior management team that has a diverse make up in terms of gender and racial mix are less likely to tolerate sexual or racial harassment. Management teams that are overwhelmingly male and white can sometimes be tolerant of behaviour that constitutes harassment as the management team may unconsciously empathise with the perpetrator rather than the victim.

So the starting point for preventing harassment is having the right management team in place that promotes and lives by a set of assumptions or shared values, one of which is that bullying and harassment is not tolerated within the organisation.

Having a management team in place that sets the correct tone, sets the appropriate standard of behaviour is the first building block.

The second building block to ensure that the workforce below the management team also buys into the organisation's standards and culture. Selecting a workforce is beyond the scope of this book, but over the years I have seen organisations that invest time and money in selection mechanisms flourish and grow. There are a whole battery of tests available that will enable an organisation to assess a prospective employee's character and emotional intelligence as well as softer skills. If those tools are available, why not use them? Furthermore getting selection processes wrong and having a higher than average staff turnover is expensive, it's an avoidable cost to the organisation.

With a positive, open, and friendly environment at work, peopled by a senior management team and workforce that exhibits and shares those characteristics and culture, bullying and harassment should not be a problem. The behavioural norm within the organisation will not tolerate that sort of behaviour. It will be second nature for those organisations to be respectful not only to one another but also to customers, suppliers and anyone else that interacts with the organisation. A positive feedback loop will develop where positive behaviour will result in positive organisational outcomes.

However just as in families or friendship groups occasionally the bad penny, the black sheep or the rotten apple slips through the net. Whilst most people are capable of change and people can turn their lives around, the truism about a leopard not changing its spots does apply more often than not. It is at that point that the policies and procedures come into play.

Ideally as part of the organisation's HR infrastructure the following procedures will be in place as a minimum:

1. A disciplinary procedure that cites bullying and or harassment as gross misconduct, with a non-exhaustive list of examples of behaviours that might amount to bullying or harassment, as well as a workable and easy to understand definition of both bullying and harassment.

2. A grievance procedure that gives employees and workers the right to redress if they think they are being bullied or harassed, with an

optional informal stage that puts the onus on the aggrieved to try to sort out the issue informally with the person who is alleged to have bullied or harassed them. Given that bullying or harassment is often an abuse of power and often involves an employee's or worker's line manager many employees or workers understandably do not feel sufficiently empowered or confident to address an issue informally and go straight to the formal stage of making a written grievance. That is fair enough and should be respected. It is not easy to address these issues informally.

Organisations with a more advanced HR infrastructure will also often have one or all of the following:

1. An induction process that sets out the organisation's standards of behaviour, that raises awareness and that leaves employees in no doubt that bullying and or harassment will not be tolerated and will be a disciplinary offence. The organisation will support and protect any employee that raises a complaint or grievance. As part of the induction employees and workers will be required to read and understand the relevant policies and procedures. Training and awareness raising are key. Further the case of Allay (UK) Limited v Gehlen UKEAT/0031/20 makes clear that training on harassment should be refreshed. To meet the defence of taking reasonably practicable steps an employer should not only train its employees when they join but also give refresher training annually.

2. An equal opportunities policy that sets out the organisation's aims and objectives of being an equal opportunities employer where ability, competence, fitness for role and application will be the key drivers in selection and promotion decisions.

3. A dignity at work policy and procedure that sets out the organisation's policy on behaviour at work. Within such a document bullying and harassment will be defined and examples of behaviours that could amount to bullying and harassment will

be given. The document should be tailored to the organisation and should be accessible and easy to understand. That dignity and harassment policy and procedure may have a different procedure for employees to lodge a complaint of harassment or bullying. The procedure will often have different steps and mechanisms to the grievance procedure and in separating out the complaints procedure from the grievance procedure

The law reflects, incentivises and rewards best practice. The statutory defence for harassment and discrimination claims are set out in the Equality Act 2010 at section 109. An employer that has taken all reasonably practicable steps to prevent harassment and other forms of discrimination will not be liable for the discriminatory and harassing acts of those in their employment.

Under the 2024 amendments employers have a positive duty to prevent harassment of a sexual nature.

The Equality and Human Rights Commission has published very useful Guidance on how to meet that duty. A failure to meet the duty will result in any award for harassment of a sexual nature being increased by up to 25%.

The Guidance in summary suggests the following 8 steps:

1. Develop an effective anti-harassment policy.

2. Engage staff by making sure all staff are aware of the policy and who to report complaints to as well as conducting one to one exit interviews to see whether harassment played a part in a person's decision to leave.

3. Assess and take steps to reduce risk. The risk assessment should be in writing and look at:

    a. Power imbalances.

   b. Lack of diversity.

   c. Whether any jobs are more insecure.

   d. Lone or night working.

   e. Customer facing roles.

   f. Alcohol consumption. This is an important one as many incidents occur after consumption of alcohol.

   g. Attendance at conferences or any event with overnight stays.

   h. Out of work social activities.

   i. Any pre-existing culture of harassment.

4. Reporting systems. Consideration should be given to using an independent reporting service and allowing reports to be anonymous.

5. Training on induction and then regular refresher training.

6. Mechanisms for dealing with a complaint.

7. Mechanisms for dealing with a complaint of third-party harassment.

8. Continual review and audit of policies and procedures to ensure they are effective.

Making out the defence is straightforward. The employer will need to show that the employee who is being accused of harassment has been inducted and trained in the organisation's procedures and policies, knows what harassment is and is well aware of the consequences of any actions that amount to harassment. If the reasonably practicable steps defence is made out then the employer will not be liable for the harassment, the employee, if named as a party to any Employment Tribunal claim will be individually liable for their own actions and will have to pay any award made by the Employment Tribunal.

It is when the issue of individual liability is explained during equal opportunities training sessions that recalcitrant employees who have been forced to attend the training by HR sit up and take notice, the arms unfold, the brows unfurrow, the ears noticeably prick up. The sound of a penny dropping in those attendees' cognitive processes is almost audible. A negative financial consequence can be a prime motivational tool – loss aversion is a well-known cognitive bias. The thought of an employee having to explain down at the Dog and Duck or worse, the family home, why they are having to cough up a substantial four or five figure sum to an employee they have harassed is one learning point the attendees usually take home from such a training session.

Changes that came into force in October 2024 impose a duty on employers to prevent harassment of a sexual nature. A failure to abide by the duty will result on any successful claim in the award being uplifted by 25%.

In summary therefore organisations can prevent bullying and harassment by:

1. Respect for each individual's dignity should be a cornerstone value of every organisation.

2. Having an organisational culture that respects the dignity of all individuals.

3. Culture means shared values and assumptions.

4. An organisation's leadership's behaviour and actions should embody the organisation's culture and values.

5. Underlying and underpinning the culture of respecting an individual's dignity should be policies that sets out the objectives, processes and procedures that support the cornerstone value of respect for the individual.

6. A risk assessment should be conducted which identifies any functions or activities which are high risk. Social events, alcohol, and overnight events carry a higher risk. Steps should be taken to mitigate identified risks.

7. A programme of training for all new starters should raise awareness of an organisation's culture, cornerstone values and expectations of behaviour of all staff. Refresher training should be provided at regular intervals.

8. Make sure that your organisation is appropriately insured, a point made in the courts both the Majarowski PFH case and the Morrisons data protection case. Whilst appropriate and full insurance will not prevent claims it will help to mitigate the damage and costs to the business.

When dealing with allegations of bullying and harassment internally a manager or supervisor should:

1. Where possible nip minor incidents of bullying and harassing behaviour in the bud before they escalate. Robust but timely intervention can be very effective,

2. Make findings of fact on each allegation. Corroborating evidence is not always necessary. Whose account is more credible?

3. Apply a sanction if necessary if the alleged conduct is found proven and amounts to bullying and harassment.

4. In more serious complaints of bullying and harassment brought internally by an employee consider the use an independent

mediator to ensure that the process is robustly independent. In many of the cases under the Protection from Harassment 1997 the courts have reminded employers that independent mediators are the better way of resolving these types of dispute rather than taking an adversarial approach by using the courts.

5. Keep policies, procedures, risk assessments under review.

Ultimately employers that foster a healthy, positive, friendly, productive working environment where senior managers set the standard of behaviour should be able to deal with any cases or incidents of poor behaviour appropriately and firmly. Those cases should be rare. Procedures, policies and training can support, re-enforce and underpin the culture. HR have a crucial role in helping to set the culture and then in monitoring and enforcing the cornerstone values.

MORE BOOKS BY LAW BRIEF PUBLISHING

A selection of our other titles available now:-

'A Practical Guide to Probation Breaches and Other Applications' by Mark Thomas
'A Practical Guide to Remarriage and Divorce' by Cordelia Williams & Claire Howard
'A Practical Guide to Privacy, Transparency, Reporting Restrictions and Closed Proceedings in the Court of Protection' by Laura Mannering
'Beaumont on Barristers – A Guide to Defending Disciplinary Proceedings (Second Edition)' by Marc Beaumont
'A Practical Guide to Payments for Environmental Services' by Ben Sharples
'A Practical Guide to the Law of Pregnancy and Maternity at Work' by Rebecca Thomas
'A Practical Guide to Redundancy – Second Edition' by Philip Hyland & Collette Moore
'A Practical Guide to International Issues for Scottish Family Lawyers' by Susie Mountain, Donna McKay, Ken MacDonald
'A Practical Guide to the Law on Deprivation of Liberty' by Ben Troke
'A Practical Guide to Rights over Airspace and Subsoil – Second Edition' by Daniel Gatty
'A Practical Guide to the Law in Relation to Inquests' by Ramya Nagesh
'A Practical Guide to the Construction and Rectification of Wills and Trust Instruments (Second Edition)' by Edward Hewitt
'A Practical Guide to Data Protection in Social Housing' by Clare Paterson
'A Practical Guide to Spousal Maintenance – Second Edition' by Liz Cowell
'A Practical Guide to International Parental Child Abduction Law (England and Wales)' by Dr Onyója Momoh
'A Practical Guide to Deprivation of British Citizenship' by Sean Ell
'A Practical Guide to Commercial Property Service Charges' by Rachel Garton
'A Practical Guide to Clinical Negligence – Third Edition' by Geoffrey Simpson-Scott (Geoff)
'A Practical Guide to the Rights of Grandparents in Children Proceedings – Second Edition' by Stuart Barlow

'The Electronic Communications Code: A Practical Guide – Second Edition' by Kerry Bretherton KC, James Castle, Mark Loveday
'A Practical Guide to the Independent School Standards – September 2023 Edition' by Sarah McKimm
'A Practical Guide to Estate Administration and Crypto Assets' by Richard Marshall
'A Practical Guide to Parental Alienation in Private and Public Law Children Cases' by Sam King QC & Frankie Shama
'Contested Heritage – Removing Art from Land and Historic Buildings' by Richard Harwood QC, Catherine Dobson, David Sawtell
'The Limits of Separate Legal Personality: When Those Running a Company Can Be Held Personally Liable for Losses Caused to Third Parties Outside of the Company' by Dr Mike Wilkinson
'A Practical Guide to Transgender Law' by Robin Moira White & Nicola Newbegin
'A Practical Guide to 'Stranded Spouses' in Family Law' by Mani Singh Basi
'A Practical Guide to Residential Freehold Conveyancing' by Lorraine Richardson
'A Practical Guide to Pensions on Divorce for Lawyers' by Bryan Scant
'A Practical Guide to Challenging Sham Marriage Allegations in Immigration Law' by Priya Solanki
'A Practical Guide to Digital Communications Evidence in Criminal Law' by Sam Willis
'A Practical Guide to Legal Rights in Scotland' by Sarah-Jane Macdonald
'A Practical Guide to New Build Conveyancing' by Paul Sams & Rebecca East
'A Practical Guide to Inherited Wealth on Divorce' by Hayley Trim
'A Practical Guide to Practice Direction 12J and Domestic Abuse in Private Law Children Proceedings' by Rebecca Cross & Malvika Jaganmohan
'A Practical Guide to Confiscation and Restraint' by Narita Bahra QC, John Carl Townsend, David Winch
'A Practical Guide to the Law of Forests in Scotland' by Philip Buchan
'A Practical Guide to Health and Medical Cases in Immigration Law' by Rebecca Chapman & Miranda Butler
'A Practical Guide to Bad Character Evidence for Criminal Practitioners by Aparna Rao
'A Practical Guide to Extradition Law post-Brexit' by Myles Grandison et al
'A Practical Guide to Hoarding and Mental Health for Housing Lawyers' by Rachel Coyle

'Stephens on Contractual Indemnities' by Richard Stephens
'A Practical Guide to the EU Succession Regulation' by Richard Frimston
'A Practical Guide to Solicitor and Client Costs – Second Edition' by Robin Dunne
'Constructive Dismissal – Practice Pointers and Principles' by Benjimin Burgher
'A Practical Guide to Religion and Belief Discrimination Claims in the Workplace' by Kashif Ali
'A Practical Guide to the Law of Medical Treatment Decisions' by Ben Troke
'Fundamental Dishonesty and QOCS in Personal Injury Proceedings: Law and Practice' by Jake Rowley
'A Practical Guide to the Law in Relation to School Exclusions' by Charlotte Hadfield & Alice de Coverley
'A Practical Guide to Divorce for the Silver Separators' by Karin Walker
'The Right to be Forgotten – The Law and Practical Issues' by Melissa Stock
'A Practical Guide to Planning Law and Rights of Way in National Parks, the Broads and AONBs' by James Maurici QC, James Neill et al
'A Practical Guide to Election Law' by Tom Tabori
'A Practical Guide to the Law in Relation to Surrogacy' by Andrew Powell
'A Practical Guide to Claims Arising from Fatal Accidents – Second Edition' by James Patience
'A Practical Guide to Asbestos Claims' by Jonathan Owen & Gareth McAloon
'A Practical Guide to Stamp Duty Land Tax in England and Northern Ireland' by Suzanne O'Hara
'A Practical Guide to the Law of Farming Partnerships' by Philip Whitcomb
'A Practical Guide to the Law of Unlawful Eviction and Harassment – Second Edition' by Stephanie Lovegrove
'A Practical Guide to Costs in Personal Injury Claims – Second Edition' by Matthew Hoe
'A Practical Guide to the General Data Protection Regulation (GDPR) – Second Edition' by Keith Markham
'A Practical Guide to Working with Litigants in Person and McKenzie Friends in Family Cases' by Stuart Barlow
'Protecting Unregistered Brands: A Practical Guide to the Law of Passing Off' by Lorna Brazell
'A Practical Guide to Secondary Liability and Joint Enterprise Post-Jogee' by Joanne Cecil & James Mehigan

'A Practical Guide to the Pre-Action RTA Claims Protocol for Personal Injury Lawyers' by Antonia Ford
'A Practical Guide to Neighbour Disputes and the Law' by Alexander Walsh
'A Practical Guide to Coercive Control for Legal Practitioners and Victims' by Rachel Horman
'A Practical Guide to the Law of Driverless Cars – Second Edition'
by Alex Glassbrook, Emma Northey & Scarlett Milligan
'A Practical Guide to TOLATA Claims' by Greg Williams
'A Practical Guide to Elderly Law – Second Edition' by Justin Patten
'A Practical Guide to Responding to Housing Disrepair and Unfitness Claims' by Iain Wightwick
'A Practical Guide to the Law of Bullying and Harassment in the Workplace' by Philip Hyland
'How to Be a Freelance Solicitor: A Practical Guide to the SRA-Regulated Freelance Solicitor Model' by Paul Bennett
'A Practical Guide to Prison Injury Claims' by Malcolm Johnson
'A Practical Guide to Advising Clients at the Police Station' by Colin Stephen McKeown-Beaumont
'A Practical Guide to Antisocial Behaviour Injunctions – Second Edition' by Iain Wightwick
'Practical Mediation: A Guide for Mediators, Advocates, Advisers, Lawyers, and Students in Civil, Commercial, Business, Property, Workplace, and Employment Cases' by Jonathan Dingle with John Sephton
'The Mini-Pupillage Workbook' by David Boyle
'A Practical Guide to Crofting Law' by Brian Inkster
'A Practical Guide to the Law of Domain Names and Cybersquatting' by Andrew Clemson
'A Practical Guide to the Law of Gender Pay Gap Reporting' by Harini Iyengar
'NHS Whistleblowing and the Law' by Joseph England
'Employment Law and the Gig Economy' by Nigel Mackay & Annie Powell
'A Practical Guide to Noise Induced Hearing Loss (NIHL) Claims' by Andrew Mckie, Ian Skeate, Gareth McAloon
'An Introduction to Beauty Negligence Claims – A Practical Guide for the Personal Injury Practitioner' by Greg Almond
'Intercompany Agreements for Transfer Pricing Compliance' by Paul Sutton
'Zen and the Art of Mediation' by Martin Plowman
'A Practical Guide to Adoption for Family Lawyers' by Graham Pegg